# CONTENTS

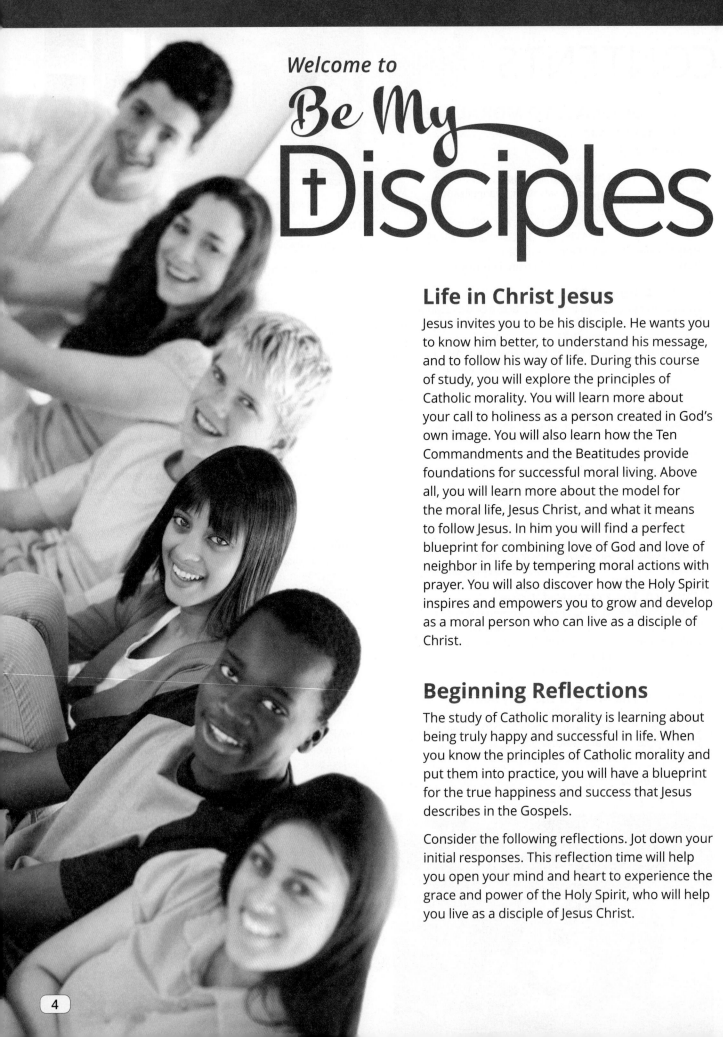

## Welcome to

# Be My Disciples

### Life in Christ Jesus

Jesus invites you to be his disciple. He wants you to know him better, to understand his message, and to follow his way of life. During this course of study, you will explore the principles of Catholic morality. You will learn more about your call to holiness as a person created in God's own image. You will also learn how the Ten Commandments and the Beatitudes provide foundations for successful moral living. Above all, you will learn more about the model for the moral life, Jesus Christ, and what it means to follow Jesus. In him you will find a perfect blueprint for combining love of God and love of neighbor in life by tempering moral actions with prayer. You will also discover how the Holy Spirit inspires and empowers you to grow and develop as a moral person who can live as a disciple of Christ.

### Beginning Reflections

The study of Catholic morality is learning about being truly happy and successful in life. When you know the principles of Catholic morality and put them into practice, you will have a blueprint for the true happiness and success that Jesus describes in the Gospels.

Consider the following reflections. Jot down your initial responses. This reflection time will help you open your mind and heart to experience the grace and power of the Holy Spirit, who will help you live as a disciple of Jesus Christ.

**1** *Approach the study of morality with faith and trust and the desire to grow in your love of God and others as Jesus taught.*

I will make wise and responsible decisions to live as a faithful follower of Jesus by

_____

_____

_____

_____

_____

_____

_____

**2** *Remember that the words of Scripture reveal that Jesus is the way, the truth, and the life.*

From my reading of Scripture, especially the Gospels, I have come to know that being a faithful disciple of Jesus demands

_____

_____

_____

**3** *Continue to grow as a person of prayer. Make the effort to work on building daily habits of prayer, especially prayer to the Holy Spirit.*

Prayer will help me make wise decisions and choices to live the new life in Christ I received in Baptism by

_____

_____

_____

_____

**4** *Listen well in class, ask questions when you do not understand, and take part enthusiastically in class activities.*

The honest effort I put into learning more about the Church's teachings on living as a follower of Christ could result in

_____

_____

_____

**5** *Work at building a well-formed conscience, build good friendships among your peers, and avoid the temptation to "follow the crowd" when your conscience tells you to do otherwise.*

I can choose to build a well-formed conscience and follow it by making wise and responsible choices. One way I can do this is by

_____

_____

_____

_____

_____

_____

_____

# GUIDE
## my FOOTSTEPS

This prayer service can be used at the conclusion of the first day of class. The leader walks at the head of a procession to the prayer area, holding the Bible high for all to see. The leader opens the Bible and places it on a table in the prayer area.

**Leader:** God our Father, you sent Jesus, your Son, to teach us the way to true happiness. By his words and example he gave us a pathway for living in harmony with you and with others. Send us the Holy Spirit to help guide our footsteps on this path to life now and forever.

**All:** **Guide me on the path that leads to you, O Lord.**

**Leader:** A reading from the Letter of Paul to the Colossians (Proclaim Colossians 3:12–15) The word of the Lord.

**All:** **Thanks be to God.**

**Leader:** Lord, when I feel bad about myself and unworthy of your love, help me to realize that I am your chosen one, holy and beloved.

**All:** **Guide me on the path that leads to you, O Lord.**

**Leader:** Lord, when I feel anger, hatred, or impatience with myself and others, help me put on compassion, kindness, humility, gentleness and patience.

**All:** **Guide me on the path that leads to you, O Lord.**

**Leader:** Lord, when I have hurt people or have been hurt by them, help me to bear with others and to learn the lessons of forgiveness.

**All:** **Guide me on the path that leads to you, O Lord.**

**Leader:** Lord, when I feel unloved and unloving, help me to put on love and to let the peace of Christ control my heart.

**All:** **Guide me on the path that leads to you, O Lord.**

**Leader:** Lord, when I feel life is too difficult and that my decisions are too hard, help me to be thankful for all that you have given me.

**All:** **Guide me on the path that leads to you, O Lord.**

**Leader:** Lord, guide us by your wisdom, strengthen us with your love, and fill us with your joy. We ask this in the name of Jesus, your Son.

**All:** **Amen.**

*Come forward and bow in reverence before the Bible.*

# Our Call to **MORAL LIVING**

**The Rich Young Man**

*Now someone approached [Jesus] and said, "Teacher, what good must I do to gain eternal life?" He answered him, ".... If you wish to enter into life, keep the commandments." He asked him, "Which ones?" And Jesus replied, "'You shall not kill; you shall not commit adultery; you shall not steal; you shall not bear false witness; honor your father and your mother'; and 'you shall love your neighbor as yourself.'" The young man said to him, "All of these I have observed. What do I still lack?" Jesus said to him, "If you wish to be perfect, go, sell what you have and give to [the] poor, and you will have treasure in heaven. Then come, follow me." When the young man heard this statement, he went away sad, for he had many possessions.* MATTHEW 19: 16-22

## What I Already Know

*Complete the following sentences.*

Holiness is . . .

_____

_____

_____

The mission of the Church is . . .

_____

_____

_____

Morality is . . .

_____

_____

_____

## Faith Vocabulary

*With a partner, take turns choosing words and defining them for each other. If there are words that neither of you can define, put a check mark next to them.*

_____ evangelization

_____ sanctifying grace

_____ Kingdom of God

_____ free will

_____ natural law

_____ Cardinal Virtues

_____ the common good

_____ social sin

## What I Want to Know

*Write a question you have under each heading.*

**Sacred Scripture**
*What has been the hardest thing for you to understand about the teachings of Jesus?*

_____

_____

_____

**The Church**
*What question do you have about Catholic moral teaching?*

_____

_____

_____

**Another Question I Have**

_____

_____

_____

**LOOKING AHEAD**
In this chapter the Holy Spirit invites you to ▶

**EXPLORE** how missionaries spread the Gospel.

**DISCOVER** how the Gospel transformed the Apostles.

**DECIDE** how you can be part of the Church's mission.

CHAPTER **1**

# The Universal MISSION

▶ Why are some people afraid to "dare to be different"?

Following Jesus is essential to being Catholic. Sometimes this means that we "dare to be different." God calls us to be part of the Church's mission by spreading the Gospel and by living the virtues of faith, hope and love. Saint Paul reminds us that to spread the Gospel we must seek God's will for us.

*Do not conform yourselves to this age but be transformed by the renewal of your mind, that you may discern what is the will of God, what is good and pleasing and perfect.*

ROMANS 12:2

▶ How do your good deeds reflect the Gospel message?

**TIMELINE**

| | c. 49 Council of Jerusalem | 397 Augustine of Hippo writes his autobiography, *Confessions*. | 1089 Church of the Holy Sepulchre in Jerusalem is rebuilt. | |
|---|---|---|---|---|
| 40 | 80 | 600 | 1200 | 1800 |

46–60 Paul's missionary journeys

1610 San Miguel Mission is built, oldest church in the continental US.

# Spreading
## the GOSPEL

**A**s followers of Jesus, we have the mission to spread the Gospel. Jesus gave the Church this mission. In his final words to the Apostles, Jesus said,

*"Go, therefore, and make disciples of all nations, baptizing them in the name of the Father, and of the Son, and of the holy Spirit, teaching them to observe all that I have commanded you. And behold, I am with you always, until the end of the age."*
MATTHEW 28: 19–20

▶ **How do you think the Apostles dared to be different?**

The mission or "job" of the Church's members is to care for one another as brothers and sisters in Christ. We do this through education, service, prayer, and the celebration of the sacraments. Though her mission is a universal one, many of us participate in the Church's mission through our local parishes.

Some members of the Church have a special calling to bring the Gospel message to people throughout all parts of the world. These important men and women are called **missionaries**.

Missionaries today have a two-fold mission. Their first mission is to establish and nurture communities of faith. Missionaries also recognize that the needs of people vary. Wherever possible, missionaries persevere on behalf of the earthly needs of people, especially in poverty-stricken areas. Missionaries give witness to Christ and the Church, while at the same time they serve the daily needs of their local communities.

▶ **In what ways are you a missionary to others in your school, parish or neighborhood?**

## Maryknoll Missionaries

The Church includes many different kinds of missionary groups. One such example is the Maryknoll missionaries.

In 1911, the U.S. bishops established the Catholic Foreign Mission Society of America, commonly known as Maryknoll. Two priests, Father James Anthony Walsh of Boston and Father Thomas Frederick Price of North Carolina, led the development of this program. The organization takes its name from its location on a hill called "Mary's Knoll" in Ossining, New York. This is where its seminary and headquarters are located.

The goal of Maryknoll is to bring the Gospel of Jesus Christ to people throughout the world. Today, Maryknoll consists of three different groups:

1. Maryknoll Fathers and Brothers,

2. Maryknoll Sisters of St. Dominic, and

3. Maryknoll Lay Missioners.

There are more than 500 priests and brothers, more than 300 sisters and about 50 lay missionaries serving the Church throughout the world.

In addition to the traditional work of missionaries, such as celebrating the sacraments, teaching and preaching, many Maryknoll missionaries work in the areas of agriculture, technology, medicine, and human rights.

▶ How are Maryknoll missionaries lights to the world?

## The Pontifical Mission Societies

For a long time, the United States was considered a "mission territory." Missionaries had to persevere due to the hostile environments of the "New World" that many European colonists also had to endure. Along with the rest of the Americas, missionaries were sent to the United States in order to spread the faith and develop dioceses and parishes.

Now the Church in the United States joins in the work of the universal Church by sending missionaries to other regions of the world to spread the Gospel. This missionary activity of the Church is accomplished through the Pontifical Mission Societies, especially the Society for the Propagation of the Faith.

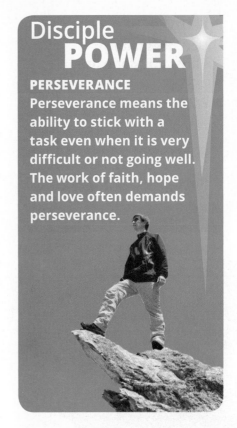

Cloister walk with Our Lady of Maryknoll statue, Maryknoll Seminary, Ossining, NY.

## FAITH JOURNAL

How must you persevere in order to share your faith in Jesus Christ?

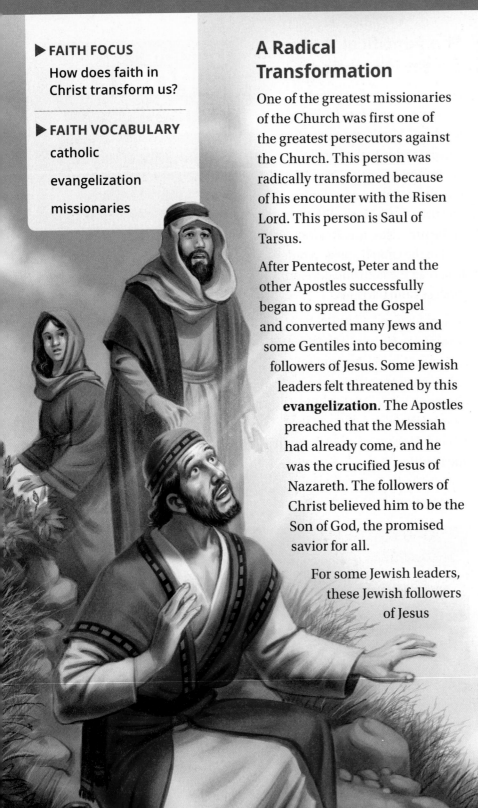

▶ FAITH FOCUS
How does faith in Christ transform us?

▶ FAITH VOCABULARY
catholic

evangelization

missionaries

## A Radical Transformation

One of the greatest missionaries of the Church was first one of the greatest persecutors against the Church. This person was radically transformed because of his encounter with the Risen Lord. This person is Saul of Tarsus.

After Pentecost, Peter and the other Apostles successfully began to spread the Gospel and converted many Jews and some Gentiles into becoming followers of Jesus. Some Jewish leaders felt threatened by this **evangelization**. The Apostles preached that the Messiah had already come, and he was the crucified Jesus of Nazareth. The followers of Christ believed him to be the Son of God, the promised savior for all.

For some Jewish leaders, these Jewish followers of Jesus were a dangerous sect within Judaism. One such person was a man named Saul. He was a devout Pharisee who was born and raised in the city of Tarsus, a place outside of Palestine. He actively persecuted the Church.

Then one day, while he was traveling to Damascus, he had a blinding vision of the Risen Lord:

*He fell to the ground and heard a voice saying to him, "Saul, Saul, why are you persecuting me?" He said, "Who are you, sir?" The reply came, "I am Jesus, whom you are persecuting. Now get up and go into the city and you will be told what you must do."*

ACTS 9: 4–6

▶ **What is the rest of Saul's story?**

Saul of Tarsus became better known as Paul, the Missionary to the Gentiles. After his conversion, Paul (which was Saul's Roman name) became one of the greatest missionaries in the early Church. He was so profoundly transformed by his encounter with the Risen Lord that he radically changed how he lived.

Paul traveled throughout the Middle East, modern-day Greece and Turkey, and as far as Rome. He proclaimed the Good News of Jesus Christ. Paul was

# The Gospel for ALL

utterly convinced that the life, Death and Resurrection of Jesus had changed everything. Through Christ's Death and Resurrection, God had offered Salvation to every person, both Jews and Gentiles. And Paul made it his mission in life to spread the Gospel by sharing his faith in Christ.

▶ What do you think compelled Paul to have such a radical change of heart?

## Peter's Vision

Faith in Christ is an ongoing journey. We need the help of the Holy Spirit to guide us in our own faith journey and in sharing our faith with others.

Peter was the first leader of the Church. And early on, he wondered whether or not belief in Christ was only for the Jews. One day he had an extraordinary vision. A Roman centurion named Cornelius had become a follower of Jesus. He came with his family to see Peter. While they were on their way, Peter had this strange vision:

*He saw heaven opened and something resembling a large sheet coming down, lowered to the ground by its four corners. In it were all the earth's four-legged animals and reptiles and the birds of the sky. A voice said to him, "Get up, Peter. Slaughter and eat."*

Acts 10:11–13

Peter knew that he could not eat all of these animals because it would have violated some Jewish dietary laws. So at first Peter did not understand the meaning of his vision.

Upon meeting with Cornelius, the Holy Spirit opened Peter's heart to understand the meaning of his vision. The Holy Spirit inspired Peter to realize that God desired all peoples to know and believe in him. Peter knew that the Church is to welcome everyone.

*Then Peter proceeded to speak and said, "In truth, I see that God shows no partiality. Rather, in every nation whoever fears him and acts uprightly is acceptable to him."*

Acts 10:34–35

▶ Why do you think Peter had a change of heart?

And so upon hearing Peter preach about Jesus, the gift of the Holy Spirit came upon the Gentiles. Cornelius and his household were all baptized in the name of Jesus (read Acts 10:44–49). God revealed to the Church that all peoples are to be saved, both the Jews and the Gentiles. And so Peter instructed the rest of the Church that they are to baptize all who believe in Jesus as Lord and Messiah.

PAVLVS·V·BVRGHESIVS·ROMANVS·PONT·MAX·

## The Growing Church

Peter realized when the Holy Spirit came upon Cornelius and other Gentiles that God desired that all peoples come to know Jesus and be saved of their sins.

Jesus' teachings were not a rejection of his Jewish faith, but the fulfillment of it. In the Sermon on the Mount, Jesus said,

> *"Do not think that I have come to abolish the law or the prophets. I have come not to abolish but to fulfill."*
>
> MATTHEW 5:17

Today we understand better how the Church developed out of a rich Jewish heritage. Jesus was Jewish. Both Mary and Joseph were Jewish. All of the Apostles and the first disciples, like Mary Magdalene, were Jewish.

Many Jewish religious rituals were assimilated into the Church's sacraments. The Apostles ate according to Jewish customs and obeyed the Law of Moses. For example, Christ instituted the Eucharist at the Last Supper, which was a Passover meal.

Because most followers of Jesus in the early Church were Jewish, their way of life resembled that of devout Jews. Yet as the Church grew and the Apostles baptized Gentiles, the way of life for members of the Church began to change. Many questions emerged on how the Church might continue to meet the needs of both Jewish Christians and Gentile Christians.

Would the Gentiles need to obey all of the Jewish dietary laws and Sabbath restrictions? Which Jewish practices must the Gentiles adhere to, and which Gentile customs might be permissible to continue? These extremely important questions needed resolution.

Jesus had formed a strong leadership in the Apostles, who were led by Peter, to deal with such things. Jesus had given the power and authority to Peter to lead the Church (read Matthew 16:18–19). Peter and the other Apostles relied on their Jewish heritage to help them. The Church formed her first council in Jerusalem to discuss and decide on how to best meet the growing needs of this now **catholic**, universal, Church.

▶ **Which issues do you think the Church resolved first?**

## The Council of Jerusalem

Even though Gentiles were accepted into the Church, there was disagreement within the leadership of the Church about which requirements and practices every member of the Church was to follow. Some leaders insisted that every member needed to follow all of the Mosaic laws, while others were concerned about demanding undue burdens upon the Gentiles.

The Church formed a council to discuss the issues. Peter listened to both sides and then declared:

*"My brothers, you are well aware that from early days God made his choice among you that through my mouth the Gentiles would hear the word of the gospel and believe. And God, who knows the heart, bore witness by granting them the holy Spirit just as he did us. He made no distinction between us and them, for by faith he purified their hearts. Why, then, are you now putting God to the test by placing on the shoulders of the disciples a yoke that neither our ancestors nor we have been able to bear? On the contrary, we believe that we are saved through the grace of the Lord Jesus, in the same way as they."*

Acts 15:7–11

This brief speech by Peter may be the single most important moment in the history of the Church. Peter, the head of the Church, was officially saying that Salvation comes from faith in Jesus Christ, and not from fidelity to Jewish customs in the Mosaic Law. The Church is unique and has a universal mission from God—to reveal to the world the love of God in Jesus Christ. From that moment on, the Church saw herself no longer as part of the Jewish religion. Christianity became distinctly different from Judaism.

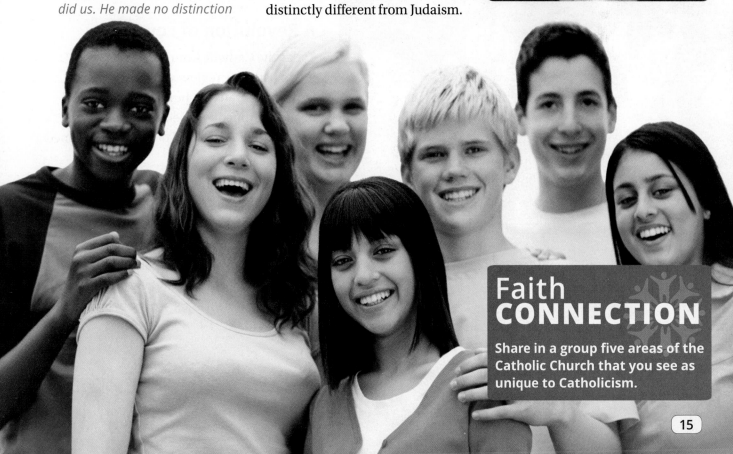

## One in Christ

The Church makes decisions that are both practical and spiritual. While the needs of every member are to be met, those needs are fulfilled through the guidance of the Holy Spirit so that all of the fundamental beliefs of the Church are upheld.

Saint Paul explained this very point in his letter to the Galatians. He wrote that every member of the Church first belongs to Christ. Faith in Jesus as Lord and Christ is essential. And in truth, the laws of Judaism were preparation for those Jews who believe in Christ (read Galatians 3:23–29).

In Christ Jesus, we have a new covenant, one that is based on an intimate relationship with him who is the Son of God. Christ removes all barriers between people, and calls each of us to be one in Christ. Paul taught,

> *For through faith you are all children of God in Christ Jesus. For all of you who were baptized into Christ have clothed yourselves with Christ. There is neither Jew nor Greek, there is neither slave nor free person, there is not male and female; for you are all one in Christ Jesus.*

GALATIANS 3:26–28

Paul was simply teaching one of the important aspects of the Church—her universal nature and mission. The Catholic Church is open to all and has as her mission to make disciples of all nations.

## A Revolution of Love

Today the Catholic Church can be found in almost every region of the world. Her faith is celebrated by hundreds of millions of people from diverse ethnic and cultural backgrounds. The Word of God is proclaimed in every major language.

Truly, the Holy Spirit is guiding the Church and transforming hearts and minds of people from every walk of life. As a revolution of love, the Church teaches that human dignity is the right of every person and that every act of love reveals the presence of God. By loving one another as God loves us, we are being lights to the world.

# A Witness for CHRIST

**You have learned about the universal mission of the Church, the sharing of God's love with all peoples.** Reflect on your role in contributing to the mission of the Church.

Your faith is not simply another part of your life. Nor is it meant to be something that you practice only for an hour on Sundays. Your faith is to be at the center of your life. Your faith is connected to the deepest part of you, your soul. God calls you to bring your faith to everything you do and to every relationship you have. God created you with the capacity to have faith, hope and love.

## YOUR VOCATION

**Every day you reveal who you are by the decisions that you make,** especially how you choose to treat others and yourself. When others hear your words and see your actions, what will they think about you? Will they know that you are a Christian by your love?

Every person has a vocation. Every Christian has a vocation to be a witness for Christ. You do not have to stand on street corners preaching the Gospel. Saint Francis of Assisi once said, "Preach the Gospel always. Use words when necessary."

▶ **In what way do you think Saint Francis' words have particular importance for today's media-rich society?**

_____

_____

# EXERCISE YOUR SOUL

**Saint Augustine of Hippo once taught** that by desiring Heaven we exercise our souls. He reminds us that each person is created both body and soul. And just as we must keep our bodies healthy, we too must keep our souls "in shape." Exercising your soul is one way you open your heart to the Holy Spirit and become transformed by love.

To be a witness for Christ you need to nurture your faith. One of the most important ways to do that is through prayer. Daily prayer is as important as daily food. Prayer can lift you up so you will persevere through the day, and prayer can help you reach out to others in need.

## A SIGN **OF FAITH**

**Wearing a religious object like a bracelet** on your wrist or a necklace around your neck can help remind you that you belong to Christ. When we proudly wear such objects they can serve to help us share our faith.

▶ **How might you use signs of your faith to evangelize others?**

## MY FAITH CHOICE

List three ways that you can help support the mission of the Church.
I will _____

_____

**PRAY** Come Holy Spirit, fill my heart with your love so that I may share with others the Good News of Jesus Christ, who is Lord and Savior of all. Amen.

## Recall

*Define each of these faith vocabulary terms:*

**1.** catholic _____

**2.** evangelization _____

**3.** missionary _____

*Choose two of the following questions, and write a short answer. Share with a partner your responses.*

**4.** What is the goal of the Maryknoll Missionaries?

_____

_____

**5.** What was decided at the Council of Jerusalem?

_____

_____

**6.** What is the universal mission of the Church?

_____

_____

## To Help You REMEMBER

1. Jesus Christ is Lord and Savior of all.

2. The Church has a universal mission to make disciples of all nations.

3. At the Council of Jerusalem, the Church respected the diversity of her members.

## Reflect

*Using what you have learned in this chapter, briefly explain this statement:*

*There is neither Jew nor Greek, there is neither slave nor free person, there is not male and female; for you are all one in Christ Jesus.*

GALATIANS 3:28

_____

_____

## Share

*As a class, look around your parish or school and identify "signs of faith" or religious objects that help express the community's Catholic faith. Share with a partner how they help you evangelize others.*

## WITH MY FAMILY

Discuss with your family ways in which you can help in the universal mission of the Church. Consider how you might utilize the Internet to spread your faith in Jesus Christ.

# Renew Your
# BAPTISMAL
## Promises

| | |
|---|---|
| **Leader:** | As we begin this course on Christian morality, let us recall our baptismal promises and rededicate ourselves to Christ. |
| | Do you renounce Satan? |
| **All:** | I do. |
| **Leader:** | And all his works? |
| **All:** | I do. |
| **Leader:** | And all his empty show? |
| **All:** | I do. |
| **Leader:** | Do you believe in God, the Father almighty, Creator of heaven and earth? |
| **All:** | I do. |
| **Leader:** | Do you believe in Jesus Christ, his only Son, our Lord, who was born of the Virgin Mary, suffered death and was buried, rose again from the dead, and is now seated at the right hand of the Father? |
| **All:** | I do. |
| **Leader:** | Do you believe in the Holy Spirit, the holy Catholic Church, the communion of saints, the forgiveness of sins, the resurrection of the body, and life everlasting? |
| **All:** | I do. |
| **Leader:** | And may almighty God, the Father of our Lord Jesus Christ, who has given us new birth by water and the Holy Spirit and bestowed on us forgiveness of our sins, keep us by his grace, in Christ Jesus our Lord, for eternal life. |
| **All:** | Amen. |

FROM THE ROMAN MISSAL, EASTER SUNDAY, RENEWAL OF BAPTISMAL PROMISES

**LOOKING AHEAD**
In this chapter the Holy Spirit invites you to ▶

**EXPLORE** how being a friend can bring happiness.
**DISCOVER** how grace helps us grow in holiness.
**DECIDE** how to build a culture of life.

CHAPTER **2**

# Human Dignity

▶ **What brings you happiness?**

Holiness and happiness are two words that often are misunderstood. Many people choose paths to happiness that end up bringing them just the opposite. Jesus inspires thousands of men and women to seek happiness through service. He taught,

*"And the king will say to them in reply, 'Amen, I say to you, whatever you did for one of these least brothers of mine, you did for me.'"*

MATTHEW 25:40

▶ **What is the connection between our search for happiness and our serving those in need?**

**TIMELINE**

| | |
|---|---|
| **1873–1897** Life of Saint Thérèse Martin of Lisieux | |
| **1964** Jean Vanier forms the first L'Arche community. | |
| **1995** Pope John Paul II teaches from *Evangelium Vitae.* | |

1850     1890     1930     1970     2000

**1905** Laïcité is formalized into French law.

**1973** US Supreme Court decides *Roe v Wade.*

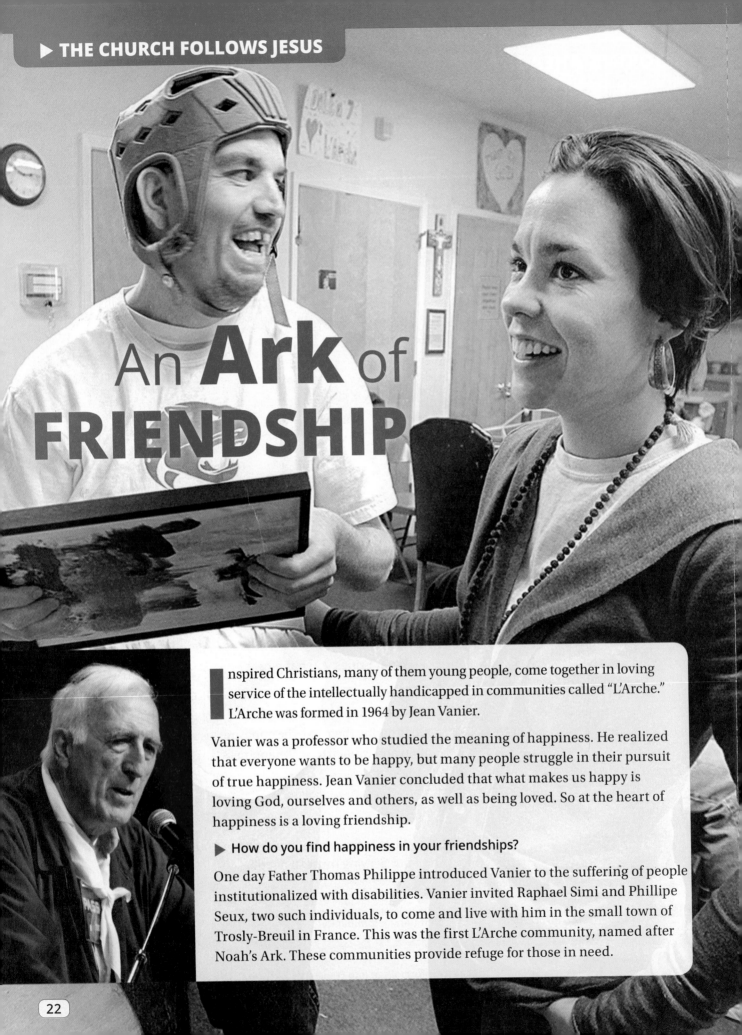

# An **Ark** of FRIENDSHIP

Inspired Christians, many of them young people, come together in loving service of the intellectually handicapped in communities called "L'Arche." L'Arche was formed in 1964 by Jean Vanier.

Vanier was a professor who studied the meaning of happiness. He realized that everyone wants to be happy, but many people struggle in their pursuit of true happiness. Jean Vanier concluded that what makes us happy is loving God, ourselves and others, as well as being loved. So at the heart of happiness is a loving friendship.

▶ How do you find happiness in your friendships?

One day Father Thomas Philippe introduced Vanier to the suffering of people institutionalized with disabilities. Vanier invited Raphael Simi and Phillipe Seux, two such individuals, to come and live with him in the small town of Trosly-Breuil in France. This was the first L'Arche community, named after Noah's Ark. These communities provide refuge for those in need.

## Share Friendship

L'Arche communities are now found in over thirty-five countries around the world. There are seventeen in the Unites States. The purpose of an L'Arche home is not to "cure" the disabled but to share friendship with them. These communities help people in need find happiness through loving friendships. And through these loving bonds, people experience an unconditional love that reflects the love that God has for us.

## The L'Arche Mission

In L'Arche homes, the intellectually challenged and the volunteers live together in community. L'Arche is not about institutional care for people; it is about solidarity through loving relationships.

The mission of L'Arche is to:

- create small communities that share their faith in an atmosphere of mutual friendship between people who have disabilities and those who desire to help people with certain disabilities.

- establish and maintain life-long support systems with people who have disabilities, especially with those who are particularly vulnerable due to old age and/ or multiple disabilities.

- enrich the lives of persons with disabilities, recognizing their unique capacity, and share the values of compassion and acceptance.

▶ What kind of values do you uphold with your friends?

## Seeds of Love

Vanier knew that persons with disabilities have dignity simply because they are children of God. In 1997, Pope John Paul II granted Jean Vanier the International Paul VI Award for extraordinary work that stems from his deep faith. The Pope said, "L'Arche has become a providential seed of the civilization of love."

## Wisdom of the Cross

What makes the L'Arche communities so extraordinary is that they demonstrate the power of Christ working through people. Many L'Arche volunteers have realized that they have come not to "save" those who are disabled, but to be "saved" by them. They find in them a special connection to Christ. Saint Paul refers to this insight as wisdom of the Cross (read 1 Corinthians 1:18–25). Wisdom of the Cross is understood when the faithful embrace suffering.

Members of L'Arche sit onstage in the Roman Colosseum after performing a play.

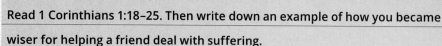

## FAITH JOURNAL

Read 1 Corinthians 1:18–25. Then write down an example of how you became wiser for helping a friend deal with suffering.

▶ FAITH FOCUS

What is true
happiness?

▶ FAITH VOCABULARY

actual grace

free will

holiness

intellect

sanctifying grace

soul

## The Gift of Grace

You might have noticed that some people tend to judge others by their outward appearances. Do a little experiment now by looking at your classmates. Do not be surprised if you first see their outward appearances.

▶ **How difficult is it for you to see beyond a person's outward appearance?**

God sees us differently. He sees the whole person from the inward to the outward—both the **soul** and the body. God looks at each of us and sees his beloved son or daughter. The prophet Isaiah compared God's love for us to that of a mother and her child. Through Isaiah, God said:

*Can a mother forget her infant,*
*be without tenderness for the*
*child of her womb?*
*Even should she forget,*
*I will never forget you.*
*See, upon the palms of my*
*hands I have written your*
*name.*          Isaiah 49:15–16

We are children of God, created in his own image and likeness (read Genesis 1:27). God shares his life with everyone—without exception. This is why every human being is sacred, or holy.

We call this gift of God sharing his life and love with us **sanctifying grace**. Sanctifying grace makes us holy, or one with God. Sanctifying grace keeps us in friendship with God. Through his grace, we participate in the life of the Trinity. The truth that God dwells in us and with us is the foundation of our dignity as human beings.

▶ **Why is human life sacred?**

# Searching for Happiness

A pilgrimage is a journey to a sacred place. The life of a Christian has also been described as a pilgrimage. We are pilgrims on an earthly journey toward the Kingdom of God. One way Christians outwardly express their spiritual journey is by making a pilgrimage. Heading toward a destination of true happiness with God is reflected in traveling to a sacred or holy place. Christians do this today as they make pilgrimages to the Holy Land, Rome, or other shrines that celebrate the mysteries of the Catholic faith.

## Joined to Christ

Christians realize that God the Father has revealed his love for us in the person of Jesus, his Son. Through the indwelling presence of the Holy Spirit, we experience God's love.

Most of you were likely baptized as infants. Your parents wanted you to honor your great dignity as a child of God. Baptism does that. Baptism brings you into the family of God, the Church. You are joined to Christ. Together as members of the Church, we walk with Jesus and each other. Your baptismal candle was lit to show that you are now in the light of Christ. You are called to be a light for others. When we share the light of Christ with others we show solidarity.

At Baptism, our life with God is restored. We receive the new life of **holiness** in Christ and the gift of the Holy Spirit. Holiness is living our life in Christ.

▶ What do you know about the celebration of Baptism?

## The Road to Happiness

From the moment of your conception, you were destined to enjoy life with God—and with others—forever. This is the very reason God created each of us.

God creates human beings with a body and a soul. The soul is spiritual and immortal. It never dies. God has also blessed you with the gifts of an **intellect** and a **free will**. The gift of your intellect is the power to know God and to reflect on how he is part of your life. The gift of free will is the ability to love and serve God and to choose to center your life on him.

We will only be happy when God is the center of our lives. When we love God, our neighbors, and ourselves, we are cooperating with God's grace. We are showing our respect for the sacredness of human life. We are traveling the road to happiness—a happiness that will last forever.

## Faith CONNECTION

Complete the sentence "Happiness is . . ." Then describe how you are on a pilgrimage of holiness.

## Love in Little Ways

From the day fifteen-year-old Thérèse Martin entered the Carmelite convent in France, she dreamed of doing great things for God. She focused on how she could keep God at the center of her life. Often Thérèse became frustrated with the difficulties of keeping God first in her life.

Then one day she read a passage from Saint Paul, in which he wrote that the best way to holiness is not by doing great things but by doing loving things (read 1 Corinthians 12:31–13:13). After reading this passage, she wrote in her journal: "O Jesus, . . . at last I have found my calling: my calling is love."

Thérèse was summarizing the Great Commandment. Jesus taught:

*"You shall love the Lord, your God, with all your heart, with all your soul, and with all your mind. This is the greatest and the first commandment. The second is like it: You shall love your neighbor as yourself. The whole law and the prophets depend on these two commandments."*

MATTHEW 22:37–40

Today we know Thérèse Martin (1873–1897) as Saint Thérèse of the Child Jesus. In 1997 Pope John Paul II named her "Doctor of the Church." Thérèse, in her own little way, was describing the way to holiness. In both your words and your actions you too are to love God with all of your heart, soul, and mind, even in the littlest of ways.

## Keeping God First

Today too many people try to find happiness in the latest gadgets, fine foods, trendy fashions, non-marital sex, or the accumulation of material possessions.

As with all earthly things, such joy is fleeting, and relationships are often damaged. Saint Augustine of Hippo (354–430) experienced many broken relationships. He finally discovered that a relationship with God is the source of true and lasting human happiness.

By choosing God first and keeping our hearts fixed on Jesus, we too will be satisfied. We will realize that striving for holiness and searching for happiness go together.

Thérèse Martin of Lisieux (1873–1897);
Augustine of Hippo (354–430)

## The Law of Love

Jesus is our model for living a holy and happy life. During his life on Earth, Jesus showed us ways to love the Father and others—even when he was ridiculed and persecuted. He taught his disciples a way to holiness and happiness in a new commandment. Jesus said,

*"I give you a new commandment: love one another. As I have loved you, so you also should love one another."*

JOHN 13:34

## Divine Help

God did not leave us on our own to figure out how to live a life of holiness and happiness. God the Father pours out the Holy Spirit upon us. The Holy Spirit constantly energizes us, directs us, and strengthens us to seek happiness by living holy lives. This divine help is called **actual grace**. Actual grace comes in many forms. This divine help empowers us to live as adopted daughters and sons of God the Father.

## Together as Church

We are not alone in our search for happiness and holiness. We are members of the new People of God, the Church. Through the gift and guidance of the Church and the celebration of the Sacraments, we are joined with Christ and with one another.

▶ Describe how the Church helps you search for holiness and happiness.

## Faith CONNECTION

List loving actions that keep your heart fixed on Jesus.

## The Beatitudes

Jesus taught about the practical connection between happiness and holiness in the Beatitudes. The Beatitudes identify the attitudes and actions blessed by God. They describe the happiness, or blessedness, of people who keep their lives focused and centered on God by committing loving acts.

Jesus taught:

*Blessed are the poor in spirit,*
*    for theirs is the kingdom of heaven.*
*Blessed are they who mourn,*
*    for they will be comforted.*
*Blessed are the meek,*
*    for they will inherit the land.*
*Blessed are they who hunger and thirst for righteousness,*
*    for they will be satisfied.*
*Blessed are the merciful,*
*    for they will be shown mercy.*
*Blessed are the clean of heart,*
*    for they will see God.*
*Blessed are the peacemakers,*
*    for they will be called children of God.*
*Blessed are they who are persecuted for the sake of righteousness*
*    for theirs is the kingdom of heaven.*

Matthew 5:3–10

The Beatitudes are a summary of discipleship. They direct our attention toward the Kingdom of God—our eternal life of happiness and holiness. To reach that goal we follow the way Jesus pointed out to us by his own teachings and through the example of his life.

## Faith CONNECTION

Reread the Beatitudes. Think about the connection between the Beatitudes, happiness, and holiness. How might you try to live one of the Beatitudes this week? How will this Beatitude help you to be happy and grow in holiness?

BEATITUDE

HAPPINESS

HOLINESS

_____

_____

_____

_____

_____

_____

_____

_____

_____

# BUILD a CULTURE of LIFE

**Every person is a sacred gift from God.** Human life is present from the moment a baby is conceived. From the moment of conception to a person's death, every person is to be cared for and treasured.

> *I have set before you life and death, the blessing and the curse. Choose life, then, that you and your descendants may live. . . .*
>
> DEUTERONOMY 30: 19

Pope John Paul II wrote an encyclical called, *Evangelium Vitae* (The Gospel of Life). In this letter, he challenged us to build a culture of life by standing up for the dignity of the human person. The Church reminds us that at the heart of Jesus' message is that all of us are to enjoy life abundantly (read John 10:10).

## PRIORITIES OF SOCIETY

**Look around your world and observe the priorities in society.** You will notice that some are contrary to the sacredness of life. Many people express opinions, make choices, and act in ways that violate human dignity or destroy human life. But God calls you to always respect and protect human life.

**Identify what you perceive to be the top three priorities in society. Then describe how these priorities do or do not build a culture of life.**

| PRIORITIES IN SOCIETY | CULTURE OF LIFE |
|---|---|
| 1. | |
| 2. | |
| 3. | |

# PRIORITIES OF THE CHURCH

**To be a follower of Christ,** you will end up going against some popular opinions about life. This could be very uncomfortable. The Catholic Church speaks out and asks you to speak out to defend all human life as sacred and to protect the dignity of each person.

As a Catholic, you are called to be pro-life "from the womb to the tomb." This means doing whatever you can to protect the life and dignity of everyone. This means recognizing the truth that human life begins at the moment of conception. Therefore, direct abortion is never an acceptable choice. This also means that we must reach out to women who struggle with their pregnancies.

Being pro-life also means having deep respect for the terminally ill and the elderly, and never abandoning them. This also means loving even our enemies and seeing that persons convicted of crimes too have dignity. Therefore, acts such as assisted suicide or the death penalty as a form of revenge are not consistent with the culture of life.

These are not easy challenges. Yet when you root your life in faith and prayer, God will give you the strength necessary to help build a culture of life.

## IN FAVOR OF LIFE

▶ Form a small group and discuss how you can speak out in favor of life as a sacred gift from God.

▶ Using art, music, or role-play, illustrate what you have discussed. Draw a rough sketch here, then complete a final work of art to show, play or demonstrate to the class.

## MY FAITH CHOICE

This week I can continue to choose life by _____

_____ .

**PRAY** Lord, help me to love others as you have loved me. Amen.

## Recall

*Define each of these faith vocabulary terms:*

**1.** sanctifying grace _____

**2.** holiness _____

**3.** soul _____

**4.** intellect _____

**5.** free will _____

**6.** actual grace _____

**7.** Beatitudes _____

**8.** solidarity _____

*Choose one of the following questions, and write a short answer. Share with a partner.*

**9.** What does it mean to say that every human being, from womb to tomb, is sacred?

_____

**10.** Describe the Christian understanding of holiness.

_____

## Reflect

*Using what you have learned in this chapter, briefly explain this statement:*

*"Man is called to a fullness of life which far exceeds the dimensions of his earthly existence . . ."*

POPE JOHN PAUL II, EVANGELIUM VITAE (THE GOSPEL OF LIFE), 2

_____

_____

## Share

*Discuss with a partner how the Beatitudes guide you in your search for happiness on Earth. Be able to explain this to a second grader.*

### To Help You REMEMBER

**1.** God created each of us in his image with a body and a soul.

**2.** We are created out of love for eternal happiness with God.

**3.** Happiness on Earth is found in our call to holiness.

## WITH MY FAMILY

Discuss as a family what truly makes your family happy. How does that happiness compare with the happiness that Jesus taught?

# The BEATITUDES

**Leader:** In the Beatitudes Jesus gives us both a vision and practical guidelines to seek and find happiness. Let us open our hearts and minds in prayer.

**All:** **Jesus, you are the way to holiness and happiness.**

**Reader 1:** Blessed are the poor in spirit, for theirs is the kingdom of heaven.

**All:** **Jesus, you are the way to holiness and happiness.**

**Reader 2:** Blessed are they who mourn, for they will be comforted.

**All:** **Jesus, you are the way to holiness and happiness.**

**Reader 3:** Blessed are the meek, for they will inherit the land.

**All:** **Jesus, you are the way to holiness and happiness.**

**Reader 4:** Blessed are they who hunger and thirst for righteousness, for they will be satisfied.

**All:** **Jesus, you are the way to holiness and happiness.**

**Reader 5:** Blessed are the merciful, for they will be shown mercy.

**All:** **Jesus, you are the way to holiness and happiness.**

**Reader 6:** Blessed are the clean of heart, for they will see God.

**All:** **Jesus, you are the way to holiness and happiness.**

**Reader 7:** Blessed are the peacemakers, for they will be called children of God.

**All:** **Jesus, you are the way to holiness and happiness.**

**Reader 8:** Blessed are they who are persecuted for the sake of righteousness, for theirs is the kingdom of heaven.

MATTHEW 5:3–12

**Leader:** Lord Jesus, you are the way, the truth, and the life. Guide us in living as you taught so we may rejoice with you, the Father, and the Holy Spirit forever in eternal happiness.

**All:** **Amen.**

**LOOKING AHEAD**

In this chapter the Holy Spirit invites you to ▶

**EXPLORE** the work of Catholic Relief Services.

**DISCOVER** the core values of Jesus' teachings.

**DECIDE** where the path of discipleship leads you now.

CHAPTER **3**

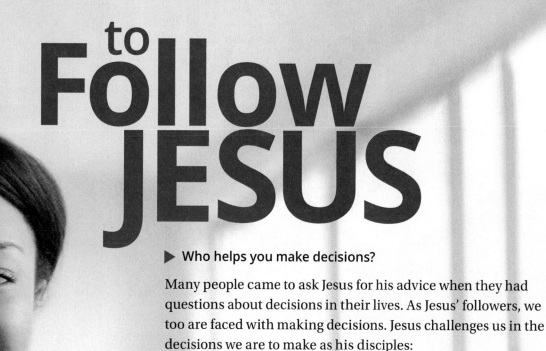

# to Follow JESUS

▶ **Who helps you make decisions?**

Many people came to ask Jesus for his advice when they had questions about decisions in their lives. As Jesus' followers, we too are faced with making decisions. Jesus challenges us in the decisions we are to make as his disciples:

*"Go, sell what you have, and give to [the] poor and you will have treasure in heaven; then come, follow me.*  MARK 10: 21

▶ **What is most challenging for you in following Jesus?**

**TIMELINE**

| | | | |
|---|---|---|---|
| **1943** U.S. Bishops initiate Catholic Relief Services. | | **1978 – 2005** Papacy of John Paul II | **1998** USCCB presents seven themes of social teaching. |

1930   1940   1950   1960   1970   1980   1990   2000

**1939 – 1945** World War II

**1964** Douglas Engelbart invents the computer "mouse."

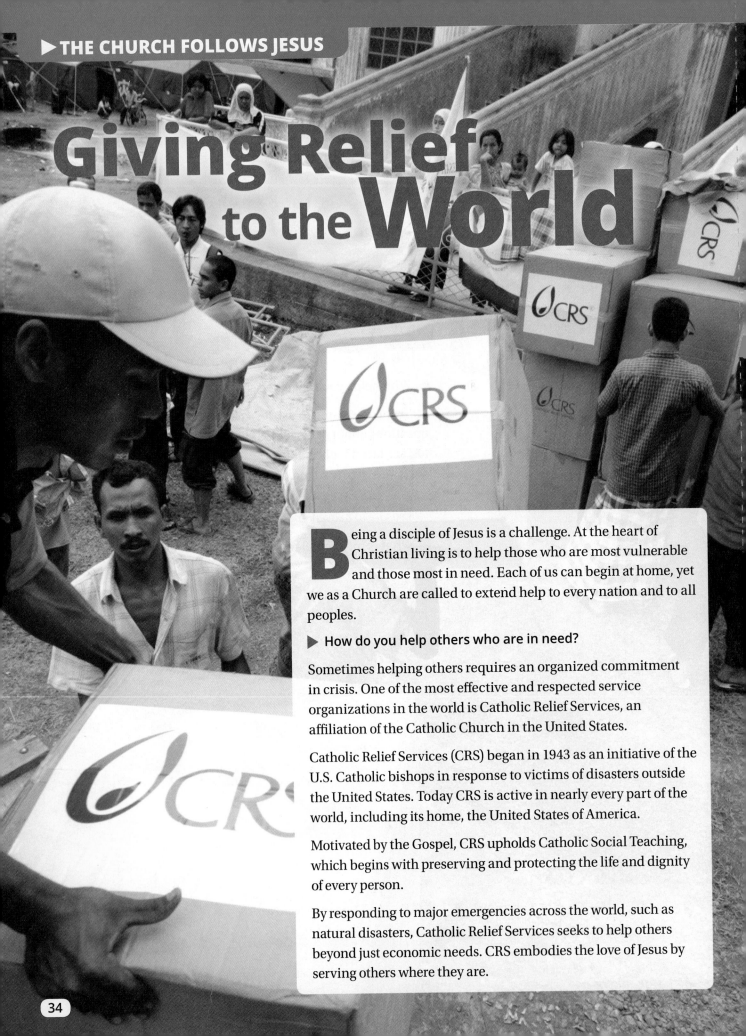

# Giving Relief to the World

**B**eing a disciple of Jesus is a challenge. At the heart of Christian living is to help those who are most vulnerable and those most in need. Each of us can begin at home, yet we as a Church are called to extend help to every nation and to all peoples.

▶ **How do you help others who are in need?**

Sometimes helping others requires an organized commitment in crisis. One of the most effective and respected service organizations in the world is Catholic Relief Services, an affiliation of the Catholic Church in the United States.

Catholic Relief Services (CRS) began in 1943 as an initiative of the U.S. Catholic bishops in response to victims of disasters outside the United States. Today CRS is active in nearly every part of the world, including its home, the United States of America.

Motivated by the Gospel, CRS upholds Catholic Social Teaching, which begins with preserving and protecting the life and dignity of every person.

By responding to major emergencies across the world, such as natural disasters, Catholic Relief Services seeks to help others beyond just economic needs. CRS embodies the love of Jesus by serving others where they are.

By fighting poverty and homelessness with a sense of nurturing justice, Catholic Relief Services continues to live out its moral responsibilities to reach out to everyone in need. Catholic Relief Services strives to help everyone live as brothers and sisters in Christ.

Working through local Catholic dioceses around the world, CRS is able to provide food, health services, education, agricultural support, and emergency responses, as well as promotes justice.

Every year some part of the world is suffering from the effects of a natural disaster. Though we are unable to prevent these events from occurring, we can takes steps to be ready for them and prevent certain disastrous consequences. This is part of CRS's mission.

## God's Superheroes

After the horrific tsunami that hit India in 2004, Catholic Relief Services worked with local dioceses to set up emergency response systems. In the Archdiocese of Pondicherry, near the southern tip of India, Catholics helped the local government set up a water buoy with tracking sensors to monitor wind speed and wave movement. This monitoring system assists local fishermen in preparing for certain climate conditions or warns them of impending dangers from the Bay of Bengal.

When the 7.0 magnitude earthquake hit Haiti in 2011, the devastation was heart breaking. Children from a Catholic Church in Kansas City, Missouri, had the strong hearts to help. Through a creative campaign, two seventh-grade friends began a fundraiser to bring hope to Haiti. With only pennies at times, their small change grew quickly into a large donation. After a weekend of Masses, two water jugs full of money became too heavy to lift. The children were asked why they decided to donate their own money to CRS. One of them said that they wanted to be God's superheroes. Through their efforts, they sought to preserve and protect lives. They loved like God.

▶ In what small ways can you make a big difference?

Through the work of Catholic Relief Services, fishermen in India were kept safe, and people in Haiti were given hope. These are just two examples of the thousands of ways in which we can give relief to the world.

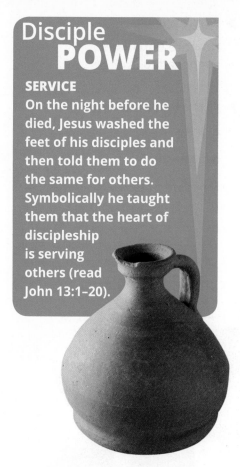

## Disciple
# POWER

### SERVICE
On the night before he died, Jesus washed the feet of his disciples and then told them to do the same for others. Symbolically he taught them that the heart of discipleship is serving others (read John 13:1–20).

# FAITH JOURNAL

Reflect on what you can do for God. How can you be one of God's superheroes?

▶ FAITH FOCUS

How are Christians supposed to live?

▶ FAITH VOCABULARY

dignity

discipleship

Kingdom of God

# Living for the KINGDOM

## The Time of Fulfillment

As is clear from the examples of Catholic Relief Services, there is always time to help others in need. In the Gospel of Mark, Jesus makes clear that now is the time for all of us to believe in him and participate in the mission of the Church:

> [Jesus said,] "This is the time of fulfillment. The kingdom of God is at hand. Repent, and believe in the gospel."
> MARK 1:15

For centuries, the Jewish people had been waiting in hope for God to send the Messiah to save them. Jesus is saying that now is the time! He is the Messiah who has come to save all people.

In Jesus, the **Kingdom of God** is breaking into the world. What is God's kingdom? It is the peace and joy of God's reign among all people. This is a reality because of what Christ has already done for us. The kingdom includes God's promise of all people living in communion with one another.

We experience a glimpse of the Kingdom when we follow Jesus by obeying his teachings. Jesus never defines the Kingdom of God. Instead, he describes different aspects of it in his teachings, such as in some of his parables. Also through his actions, Jesus gives witness to the kingdom. At the heart of Christian **discipleship** is living for God's kingdom, which means following Jesus in word and in deed.

▶ How is living for God's kingdom related to helping others in need?

## Love of God and Neighbor

Christians believe that Jesus is the Messiah, the Savior, and the Son of God. Jesus lived as a devout Jew. He studied the Torah, the first five books of the Bible, and followed the Ten Commandments.

One day, a man asked Jesus which law was the most important. Jesus gave the man this response:

> "The first is this: 'Hear, O Israel! The Lord our God is Lord alone! You shall love the Lord your God with all your heart, with all your soul, with all your mind, and with all your strength.' The second is this: 'You shall love your neighbor as yourself.' There is no other commandment greater than these."
> MARK 12:29–31

Jesus combined two commandments into one, making love of God and love of neighbor inseparable. So living for the kingdom means that we are to love both God and our fellow human beings. Living for the Kingdom of God is the mission of the Church.

▶ How is loving others loving God?

## Importance of Prayer

Being a disciple involves having a personal relationship with God. This involves loving God first. You can grow in your relationship with God through both prayer and loving acts.

Prayer gives direction to our loving actions. In prayer we often realize the challenge of Jesus' teachings on who our neighbors are. Our neighbors are people with whom we come in contact.

▶ How and when do you pray?

## Love without Limit

For many Christians, the most challenging part of Jesus' commandment is to love our neighbors, including those who do not like us. This becomes apparent when Jesus taught,

> "But I say to you, love your enemies, and pray for those who persecute you, that you may be children of your heavenly Father, for he makes his sun rise on the bad and the good, and causes rain to fall on the just and the unjust."
>
> MATTHEW 5:44–45

Yet how is this even possible? Why does Jesus insist on us loving even our enemies? Are not our enemies the people who are against us? Jesus challenges us to have a different attitude. Jesus calls us to love without boundaries, without prejudices, without limit.

Think of the following example: What if there is a bully in school who picks on you or a friend? Feeling upset or angry is natural and okay. How you deal with your anger is what Jesus is focused on. Being angry is not the same thing as being hateful. Hating is when you wish something bad happens to someone.

Jesus knows that loving that bully may not be easy. Nonetheless, you are to show love to all. Showing love toward our enemies may mean telling them to stop, or trying to keep yourself or your friend protected. Or you might even respond to someone's nasty behavior with kind behavior. Jesus insists that we should never let someone else's wrong or unjust actions lead us to commit wrong or unjust actions ourselves. As disciples, we are to do and say what is always true, good and beautiful. This is how we love without limit.

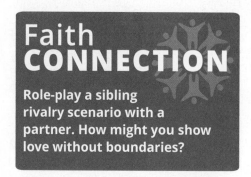

# Faith CONNECTION

Role-play a sibling rivalry scenario with a partner. How might you show love without boundaries?

## The Good Hero

One of Jesus' most well-known parables was about loving one's enemy. This parable was about the Good Samaritan. In Jesus' time, Samaritans and Jews hated each other, so Jesus took the hated enemy and made him the hero of this parable.

*"But a Samaritan traveler who came upon him was moved with compassion at the sight. He approached the victim, poured oil and wine over his wounds and bandaged them. Then he lifted him up on his own animal, took him to an inn and cared for him. The next day he took out two silver coins and gave them to the innkeeper with the instruction, 'Take care of him. If you spend more than what I have given you, I shall repay you on my way back.' Which of these three, in your opinion, was neighbor to the robbers' victim?" He answered, "The one who treated him with mercy." Jesus said to him, "Go and do likewise."*

Luke 10:33–37

## See as God Sees

Loving enemies requires God's grace. Think of someone that you have a hard time loving and pray for him or her every day for a week. Try to see them the way that God sees them.

How can we see others, let alone our enemies, as God sees them? To see as God sees, we are first to acknowledge others according to their **dignity**. Every person is created by God in his image and likeness. Therefore, every person deserves to be treated with respect, as the Good Samaritan did for the man beaten on the side of the road.

Because each of us is created in the image and likeness of God, every person has dignity. And from the dignity of every person flows a series of principles that are to guide our actions. At the heart of these principles are the teachings of Jesus. First, to love God includes loving our neighbors, including our enemies. Secondly, we are to love one another as God loves us (read John 13:34). This is why love of God and love of neighbor are inseparable.

▶ How did the Good Samaritan love like God?

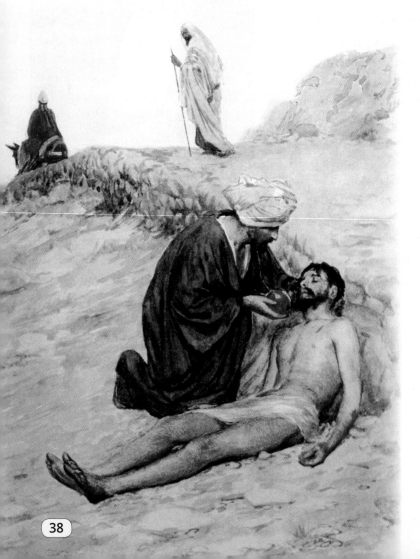

*The Good Samaritan,*
William Henry Margetson

## Love like God

Loving like God is not easy, but each of us is capable of love. Jesus challenges us to believe in the Gospel because his way is how we can love like God.

The word *gospel* literally means "good news." The Good News or Gospel message is that Jesus shows us the way to love like God. And when we love like God, we live for the Kingdom of God.

Jesus proclaims in the Gospel that God offers forgiveness and reconciliation to all sinners. And this is part of how we love like God. We start by recognizing that we need God. One of the worst things we can do is deny our own sinfulness and our need for God's mercy. Jesus told us that he came for sinners:

> *"Those who are well do not need a physician, but the sick do. I did not come to call the righteous but sinners."* Mark 2:17

If we are to prepare for the kingdom, we must recognize that Jesus, the King, has come to save us from sin. We then can begin to reconcile our relationships with God and experience his loving mercy.

## Forgiveness

The Gospel of Luke tells us a great story about Jesus and forgiveness.

> *Jesus said to [a Pharisee] in reply, "Simon, I have something to say to you." "Tell me, teacher," he said. "Two people were in debt to a certain creditor; one owed five hundred days' wages and the other owed fifty. Since they were unable to repay the debt, he forgave it for both. Which of them will love him more?" Simon said in reply, "The one, I suppose, whose larger debt was forgiven." He said to him, "You have judged rightly."* Luke 7:40–43

Jesus told Simon the Pharisee this parable because Simon did not realize his need for God's mercy. Simon focused only on the sins of others. A sinful woman showed great love to Jesus by washing his feet with her tears and anointing his feet with oil. Jesus had forgiven her many sins because she had shown great love for him. Though she had sinned, she knew she needed God's mercy. Her love for Jesus demonstrated her faith in God.

## Faith CONNECTION

Is there someone to whom you need to apologize? Is there someone you need to forgive? Bring both of those needs to prayer, and then act.

## With Great Love

Sometimes seeking forgiveness is as difficult as giving forgiveness. Jesus shows us not only the path of forgiveness, but also the way to compassion.

This way to compassion is hard for us because it often asks us to move outside of our "comfort zones." We might be afraid of people who are different than us, or we might think we will be asked to go beyond our abilities.

Jesus helps us past those fears, and reaches out to all peoples, especially those who are ignored, rejected or abandoned. Jesus showed compassion to everyone, whether the person was a leper, a blind man, a woman who lost her son, an adulteress about to be killed, a young boy possessed by a demon, or a paralytic. Jesus revealed a heart of compassion and challenges us to be people of compassion.

The ultimate challenge from Jesus is that our concern for those in need will be the basis for God's judgment:

Mother Teresa at her mission to aid poor and starving people in Calcutta, India

*"When the Son of Man comes in his glory, and all the angels with him, he will sit upon his glorious throne, and all the nations will be assembled before him. And he will separate them one from another, as a shepherd separates the sheep from the goats. He will place the sheep on his right and the goats on his left. Then the king will say to those on his right, 'Come, you who are blessed by my Father. Inherit the kingdom prepared for you from the foundation of the world. For I was hungry and you gave me food, I was thirsty and you gave me drink, a stranger and you welcomed me, naked and you clothed me, ill and you cared for me, in prison and you visited me.' Then the righteous will answer him and say 'Lord, when did we see you hungry and feed you, or thirsty and give you drink? When did we see you a stranger and welcome you, or naked and clothe you? When did we see you ill or in prison, and visit you?' And the king will say to them in reply, 'Amen, I say to you, whatever you did for one of these least brothers of mine, you did for me.'"*

MATTHEW 25:31–40

Jesus was clear that the way we show love to others is how we show love for him. This often includes even the littlest of things we do. Mother Teresa is remembered for pointing out that we should do "small things with great love."

▶ **What "small thing" can you do for someone in need?**

# The DEMANDS of LOVE

**Following Jesus means loving both God and neighbor.** We are called to love one another as God loves us. And loving like God is loving without limits. Love demands seeking God's mercy. Love demands reaching out to those most in need with forgiveness and compassion.

Being a disciple of Jesus involves discipline. This habit of discipline means self-control and being focused on what is true, good and beautiful. Even artists, musicians and athletes recognize the need for discipline, and this comes with practice. Christian discipline takes the practice of love—love for God, others and ourselves.

## LOVING GOD

**Loving God means that we enter into a relationship with him, and this love demands prayer.** As a disciplined disciple, you reserve time for prayer. For each step below, describe how you are already practicing prayer in that way:

| DISCIPLINED STEPS | PRACTICING PRAYER |
|---|---|
| Form the habit of morning prayer. | _____ |
| Say a brief prayer before each meal. | _____ |
| Pause during the day just to talk with God. | _____ |
| At night, reflect on how you loved God that day. | _____ |
| Participate in Mass each Sunday. | _____ |

# LOVING OTHERS

**Love is a choice, a devotion, a commitment.** Each of us has a loving commitment to those most dear to us. There is love of family, which is a natural bond, though not always easy. This love for parents and siblings is your first "school of love." With your family you can "practice" love in a caring environment.

There is also love of friends. We are born into a family, but we choose our friends. Good friends bring out the best in us. They like and respect us for who we are.

**Identify how your family and friends have helped you practice love.**

_____

_____

_____

# LOVING ONESELF

**This may sound odd, but God wants us to love ourselves.** Love of oneself is not the same as being conceited. It is quite the opposite. Love of oneself is a self-respect based on the simple truth: you are a child of God and he loves you unconditionally.

▶ Are your decisions ones that respect who you are as God's child? How might you improve your self-respect?

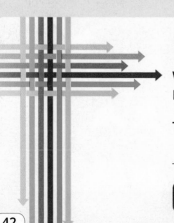

## MY FAITH CHOICE

Whose love for you has made a huge difference in your life? How does that love for you imitate God's love for all of us?

This week I can continue to choose love by _____

_____

**PRAY** *"Lord, help me to love others as you love me. Amen."*

## Recall

*Define each of these faith vocabulary terms:*

**1.** Kingdom of God _____

**2.** discipleship _____

**3.** dignity _____

*Choose two of the following questions, and write a short answer. Share with a partner.*

**4.** What did Jesus say is the greatest commandment?

_____

_____

**5.** Why did Jesus make the Samaritan the hero of his parable?

_____

_____

**6.** According to Jesus, how will God judge us?

_____

_____

## Reflect

*How can others see that you believe in the Gospel of Jesus Christ? Write your thoughts in this space or in your journal.*

_____

_____

_____

_____

## Share

*Work with a partner ar small group. Choose a parable of Jesus. Create a modern day version to show how you can echo Jesus' message of discipleship today. If time allows, share it with your class.*

## WITH MY FAMILY

As a family, discuss who in your neighborhood or community is in need. Perhaps it is a child with special needs or a single parent or senior citizen. Discuss how you might respond to the need.

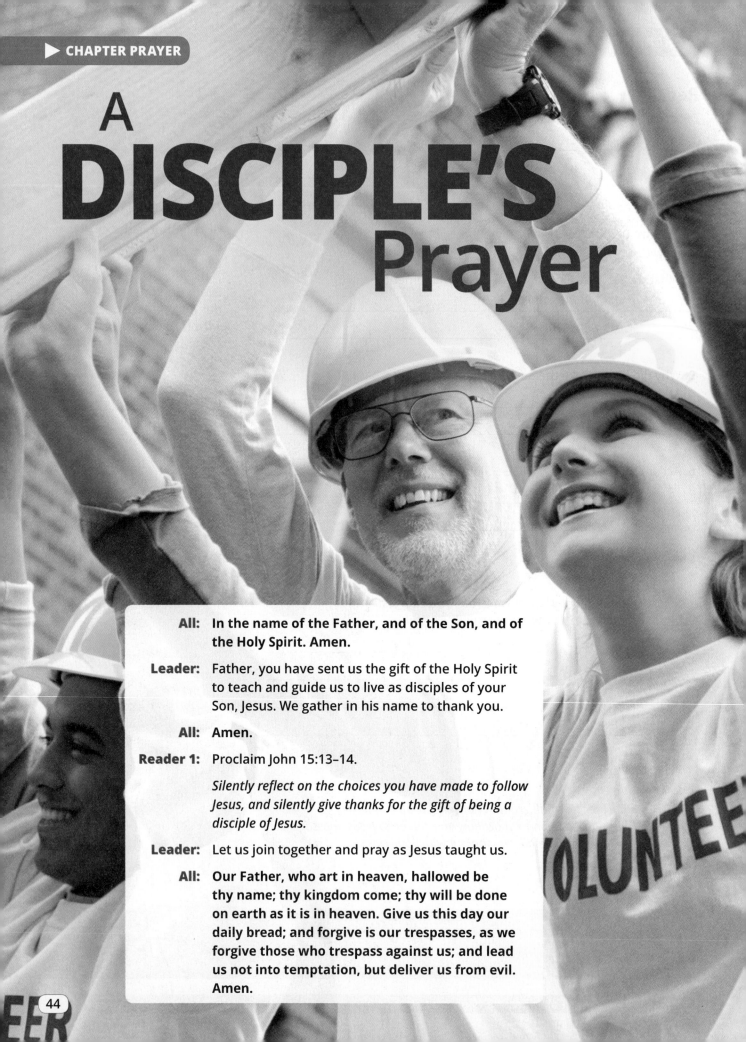

# A DISCIPLE'S Prayer

**All:** In the name of the Father, and of the Son, and of the Holy Spirit. Amen.

**Leader:** Father, you have sent us the gift of the Holy Spirit to teach and guide us to live as disciples of your Son, Jesus. We gather in his name to thank you.

**All:** Amen.

**Reader 1:** Proclaim John 15:13–14.

*Silently reflect on the choices you have made to follow Jesus, and silently give thanks for the gift of being a disciple of Jesus.*

**Leader:** Let us join together and pray as Jesus taught us.

**All:** Our Father, who art in heaven, hallowed be thy name; thy kingdom come; thy will be done on earth as it is in heaven. Give us this day our daily bread; and forgive is our trespasses, as we forgive those who trespass against us; and lead us not into temptation, but deliver us from evil. Amen.

LOOKING AHEAD
In this chapter the Holy
Spirit invites you to ▶

**EXPLORE** how one man followed his conscience.
**DISCOVER** how Gospel values properly form your conscience.
**DECIDE** on how you will make good moral choices.

CHAPTER **4**

# GUIDED by Conscience

▶ **Who helps you make decisions?**

Our voluntary actions come from the decisions we make. And these actions are often a reflection of the values we treasure the most. As you mature, you will have to make more decisions on your own. If you choose to make good moral decisions, you will shine before others because you are following Christ, who is the Light of the world. That is why he said,

*"You are the light of the world. A city set on a mountain cannot be hidden. Nor do they light a lamp and then put it under a bushel basket; it is set on a lampstand, where it gives light to all in the house. Just so, your light must shine before others, that they may see your good deeds and glorify your heavenly Father."*

MATTHEW 5:14-16

▶ **What are some choices you have made to show that your light is shining before others?**

**TIMELINE**

| | | | |
|---|---|---|---|
| **1801–1890** Life of John Henry Newman | **1917–1980** Life of Óscar Romero | **2007** USCCB publishes *Forming Consciences for Faithful Citizenship.* | |

1770　1800　1830　1860　1890　1920　1950　1980　2010

**1791** US Bill of Rights is ratified.

**1962** Nick Holonyak Jr invents the first LED.

# Voice of the Voiceless

**H**ave you ever had someone tell you to follow your conscience? This is very good advice, but it can be easily misunderstood. Following your conscience does not mean to do whatever you feel is right at the moment. Instead, to follow one's conscience means to do whatever God would have us do in faithfully following his Commandments. To follow one's conscience means to do what is right. Often, following one's conscience is very difficult, and sometimes it is life-threatening.

Óscar Arnulfo Romero was a Catholic priest who followed his conscience and did what is right. In the late 1970s, as the archbishop of San Salvador, Romero chose to confront the horrific conditions the people of El Salvador endured. Archbishop Romero was often threatened with death because he spoke for the poor and against the abusive government, but he refused to back down. His conscience was something that he could not ignore. He had been noted as saying that his faith and conscience insisted that he become the "voice of the voiceless" in El Salvador.

## Support for the Poor

During this time El Salvador was a very poor country in which most of the people had little land and few rights. Many of the priests in El Salvador began to work with the poor, and some encouraged the people to organize in order to claim their basic human rights. Archbishop Romero was at first very cautious about how to approach and confront the issues. He knew that the Catholic Church is a church for all people, no matter their economic status in society, or political influence in the government. Yet in El Salvador the Church was under attack, and many Catholic priests, including his friend Father Rutilio Grande, were assassinated because of the Church's support for the poor and vulnerable. Archbishop Romero witnessed the suffering and martyrdom of people who, out of love for God and others, gave their own lives to be lights of Christ to the world.

Archbishop Romero began to recognize that he too had to act on behalf of the poorest of the poor. He had to do what he could to help those in need and those in danger. He needed to work for justice out of love, even if it meant he might suffer.

## Suffering Love

For Archbishop Romero, "follow your conscience" meant a deep commitment to live as Jesus lived. Jesus always gave a preference to serving and helping the poorest people whom he encountered. So

Archbishop Romero helped the people of El Salvador protect and defend their basic human rights, even when it was against unjust government policies.

On March 24, 1980, the Archbishop was shot and killed while celebrating Mass in a chapel at the hospital called "La Divina Providencia." Days before his murder, the Archbishop told a reporter, "You can tell the people that if they succeed in killing me, that I forgive and bless those who do it. Hopefully, they will realize that they are wasting their time. A bishop will die, but the church of God, which is the people, will never perish."

More than 250,000 people came to his funeral, and thousands visit San Salvador each year on his memorial to honor his life. In 1997 he was formally recognized by Pope John Paul II as "Servant of God." This officially opened his cause for canonization. Archbishop Óscar Romero is revered by thousands of people in Latin America for his devout faith, courageous conscience, and suffering love for the poor.

# FAITH JOURNAL

How can you give "voice" to the "voiceless" in your community?

▶ **FAITH FOCUS**

How is Christian morality a path to freedom?

▶ **FAITH VOCABULARY**

conscience

morality

natural law

sin

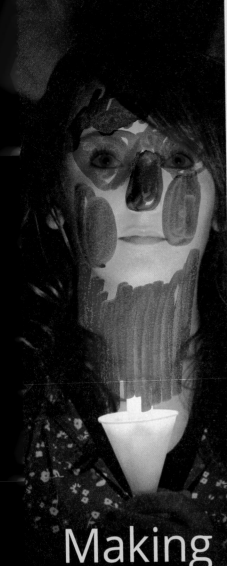

## Lights in the World

Christian **morality** is the way of living for those who have been joined to Christ, the Light of the world, in Baptism. This way of life has been revealed to us by God and is based on the following:

- **The life and teachings of Jesus Christ.** Jesus is the fulfillment of the Covenant. In him and through his teachings, we learn to understand that we are to love as God loves.

- **The teachings of the Church.** As the Holy Spirit works through the Church, we come to better understand with the aid of the Magisterium how we are to live according to God's Laws.

- **Sacred Scripture.** Through the story of the Covenant, we learn that God leads us to align our wills with his.

▶ What have you learned from these sources about what is good and true?

For the followers of Jesus, living a moral life is not simply about following a long list of rules. The Christian moral life is more about freely responding to God the Father, and the Son, and the Holy Spirit.

## True Freedom

Free will and reason make us responsible for our own intentional actions. They give us the power to know and choose between what is good and what is evil. They give us the power to bring either light or darkness to the world. The Scriptures remind us:

> *If you choose you can keep the commandments; it is loyalty to do his will.* Sirach 15:15

Certain factors can impact both your freedom to choose and the responsibility for your choices. Some young people have grown up in unhealthy families or communities. Such factors may diminish a person's culpability, or responsibility, for any given action.

Through a life of prayer, reading Scripture, especially the Gospels, and learning the teachings of the Church, we strive to live as lights in our world. With the Holy Spirit's grace, we can know and do what is good, and recognize and reject what is evil.

One of our inalienable rights as human beings is the right to exercise freedom, especially in religious and moral matters. Without this freedom, we would not be able to give ourselves to God and freely accept his gift of himself to us. True freedom enables us to make good moral decisions, even to the point of suffering for the sake of others.

▶ How is doing whatever you feel like doing restrictive?

## Making
# Moral Decisions

## Wages of Sin

Paul taught in his letter to the Romans that being "not under the law but under grace" does not mean we can do anything we like. Saint Paul was affirming how blessed we are:

> For sin is not to have any power over you, since you are not under the law but under grace. What then? Shall we sin because we are not under the law but under grace? Of course not!
> . . . For the wages of sin is death, but the gift of God is eternal life in Christ Jesus our Lord.
>
> ROMANS 6:14–15, 23

The grace of the Holy Spirit has been given to us. The Holy Spirit helps us know how to live as children of God and gives us the strength to freely choose to live our lives as Christ taught us.

In the face of all we have been taught, we nevertheless sometimes freely and knowingly do what is against God's Law. When we do, we **sin**. Sin sets us apart from and against God. Sin turns our hearts away from his love.

**Mortal Sin.** The Church uses the term *mortal sin* to describe serious sins. The word *mortal* means "deadly." A mortal sin causes the loss of sanctifying grace because we have chosen to reject God.

Without grace, we have no eternal life with God.

Unrepented mortal sin brings eternal death. We can, of course, find forgiveness for our mortal sins and restore our lives with God through the Sacrament of Penance and Reconciliation.

**Venial Sin.** Some sins involve a less serious offense against God. Venial sin does not cause the loss of sanctifying grace. Sins are venial when (1) we do something wrong that is in itself not gravely, or seriously, evil; or (2) we do not have full knowledge of the act's sinfulness; or (3) we do not have complete freedom in making our choice. We should not take venial sins lightly. The idea that they are less serious does not mean that it really does not matter that we commit them.

All sins turn our hearts away from God's love. Getting into the habit of committing venial sins can set us up to sin more seriously.

**Sins of omission.** We can also commit a sin by doing nothing. These sins are called sins of omission. If a person is aware of something that is morally good and is able to act but chooses not to, then that person has committed a sin of omission.

## Daily Choices

Living our life in Christ is a daily, lifelong choice. Living our life in Christ takes place right here, right now. We need to deal with the moral issues that meet us face-to-face each day.

▶ **How do you know that you are on the right track?**

## The Natural Law

Imagine that you find a wallet in the hall at school. It has twenty dollars in it and a student identification card. What would you do? Would you make sure that the owner got the wallet and money back? It does not take a saint to know what to do in this situation. There is only one right thing to do: You do not take what does not belong to you; you return the wallet.

God has placed within us the ability to know the **natural law**. This means that through our ability to reason we can understand that we are to do good and avoid evil.

The natural law is the foundation of the moral life for everyone, Christian or not. God put order in all of creation, including our actions. God established and set forth what is right, good and beautiful because he is the Creator. Then he gave us the ability to know what is right and what is wrong, and the ability to freely choose to act virtuously or to commit sin.

This moral order in the world is knowable by reason. For example, anyone who properly uses his or her reason can understand that murder is wrong. To intentionally kill an innocent person violates the person's fundamental right to life. Furthermore, a murderer disrespects the innocent person's inherent, or natural, dignity as well as his or her own.

The natural law is also evident by the common universal moral norms and laws that various civilizations have established and upheld, from ancient Babylonian times with the Code of Hammurabi to the United States of America with the Bill of Rights. Even the Hippocratic Oath, dating back to 5th Century BC Ancient Greece, continues to be upheld by many modern doctors today.

▶ **Which universal moral norms can you list?**

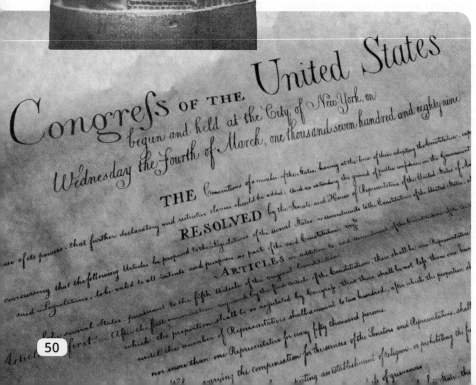

Law Code of Hammurabi, King of Babylon, detail of stele. Louvre Museum, 1792-1750 BC. (foreground)

U.S. Bill of Rights, detail of the Preamble. National Archives. (background).

## Elements of Moral Actions

The moral life we live is formed by the choices we make. The person who commits an intentional act is called the agent. The goodness or evil of our actions depends on three things. These are:

- **What we choose to do.** This is called the object of the moral act. It is what the agent knowingly chooses to do or not to do. Some examples of intrinsically evil acts are: adultery, murder, lying, and theft.

- **Why we choose.** This is called the intention of the moral act. The agent's intention, or motive, for choosing a moral act affects the goodness or evil of an act. A good intention can never turn an evil act into a good act because an intrinsically evil act, regardless of intention, is always evil.

  A bad intention, however, can turn a good act into an evil one. For example, you go out of your way to compliment your teacher. You do this only because you want this teacher to write a letter of recommendation for you. The compliment is a good act; the letter is a good end. Your motive is tainted; so too is the act.

- **The details surrounding the act.** We call these the circumstances of the moral act. The circumstances include the how, who, when, and where of the act. Such circumstances can increase or lessen the agent's culpability and also give evidence to the severity of the evil or diminish the goodness. For example, if the agent committed an evil act out of fear, the responsibility might be lessened. And stealing twenty dollars is not as severe as stealing twenty million dollars. Often the severity of the evil act can relate to the severity of the agent's responsibility.

## The Gift of Conscience

Christian life is made up of many choices. Within us, a persistent "voice" helps us make good moral choices. We call this voice the **conscience**.

God created every human being with a conscience. It helps a person judge right from wrong. A well-formed conscience helps a person to see one's thoughts and actions more clearly. Whether he or she is about to do something, or is in the process of acting, or even has finished the act, the conscience is at work in the person.

Our conscience is a gift from God that help us make the right decisions to live our life according to God's will. It guides us in our attitudes, our actions, and our choices.

When you honestly work at building a well-formed conscience and follow it, you are building a guide that, with the Holy Spirit's help, will lead you toward God and eternal happiness.

## Faith CONNECTION

Using the two panels provided here, sketch a cartoon-like illustration in which "Conscience" is a character who is helping a friend make a decision.

# In THE RIGHT DIRECTION

**You are constantly making decisions that not only have an effect on you but also on other people.** To help you make the right moral decisions, you need to develop a well-formed conscience. This is very important since you have the responsibility to obey your properly formed conscience. And a well-formed conscience will help keep you in the right direction.

# A WELL-FORMED CONSCIENCE

**Making the right choice is not always easy,** but a well-formed conscience and the grace of the Holy Spirit will help you do so. Usually, you make a certain choice because you think it will make you happy. A well-formed conscience can help you examine whether that choice is a responsible Christian decision or if that choice will harm you or other people. Here are some steps to help you develop a well-formed conscience:

- **Always think before you act.** God gave you the gift of reason so you can know what is true, good and beautiful.

- **Remember the choices Jesus made.** You have heard about and read about the choices Jesus made in the Gospels. Read some of these Gospel stories again.

- **Pray to the Holy Spirit.** Open your mind and heart to the grace of the Holy Spirit to guide you in making wise and responsible choices.

- **Remember the teachings of the Catholic Church.** The Church is our Mother and Teacher. She teaches us how to be a faithful follower of Jesus.

- **Receive the sacraments.** Take part in the celebrations of Penance and Reconciliation and Eucharist often and regularly.

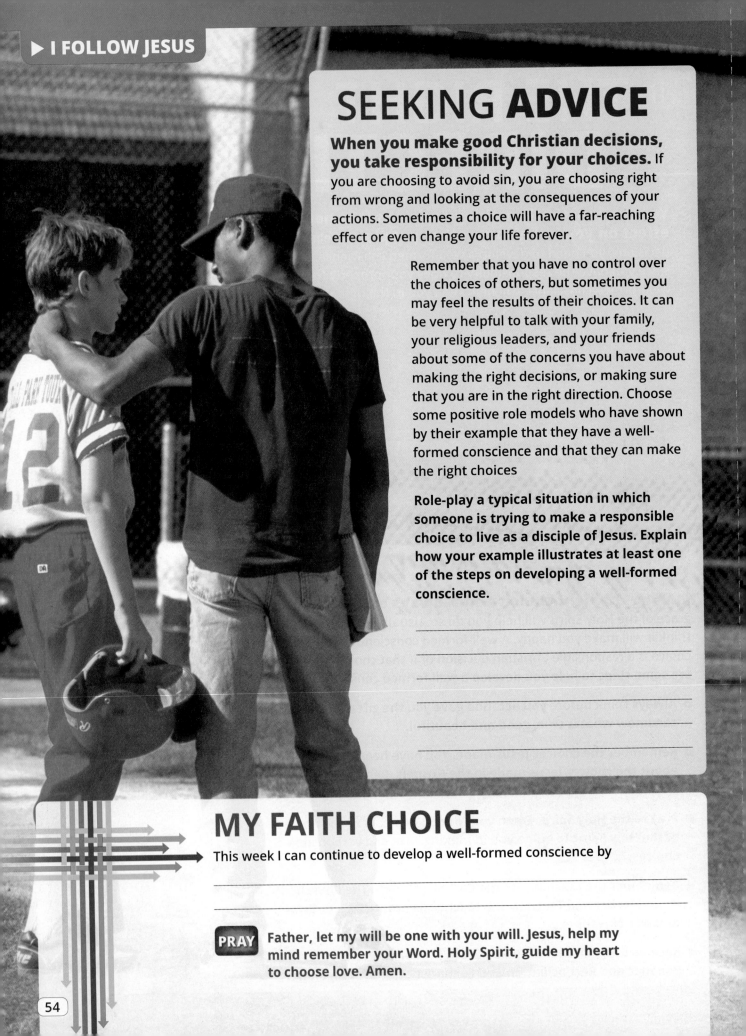

# SEEKING **ADVICE**

**When you make good Christian decisions, you take responsibility for your choices.** If you are choosing to avoid sin, you are choosing right from wrong and looking at the consequences of your actions. Sometimes a choice will have a far-reaching effect or even change your life forever.

Remember that you have no control over the choices of others, but sometimes you may feel the results of their choices. It can be very helpful to talk with your family, your religious leaders, and your friends about some of the concerns you have about making the right decisions, or making sure that you are in the right direction. Choose some positive role models who have shown by their example that they have a well-formed conscience and that they can make the right choices

**Role-play a typical situation in which someone is trying to make a responsible choice to live as a disciple of Jesus. Explain how your example illustrates at least one of the steps on developing a well-formed conscience.**

_____

_____

_____

_____

_____

_____

# MY FAITH CHOICE

This week I can continue to develop a well-formed conscience by

_____

_____

**PRAY** Father, let my will be one with your will. Jesus, help my mind remember your Word. Holy Spirit, guide my heart to choose love. Amen.

# Recall

*Define each of these faith vocabulary terms:*

**1.** conscience _____

**2.** morality _____

**3.** mortal sin _____

**4.** natural law _____

**5.** venial sin _____

*Choose one of the following questions to answer, and write a short answer. Share with a partner.*

**6.** Describe the sources of Morality.

_____

_____

**7.** Describe the steps in developing a well-formed conscience.

_____

_____

## To Help You REMEMBER

**1.** Christian morality is how we live our lives as disciples of Jesus.

**2.** We are called to form our consciences with faith and reason.

**3.** Christian morality is rooted in the teachings of the Church.

# Reflect

*Using what you have learned in this chapter, briefly explain this statement:*

> *"[Conscience] is a messenger of him, who, both in nature and in grace, speaks to us from behind a veil."*
>
> JOHN HENRY NEWMAN, "LETTER TO THE DUKE OF NORFOLK" (1885)

_____

_____

_____

# Share

*Discuss with a partner the meaning of the adage, "Let your conscience be your guide." Share examples of how a well-formed conscience can guide a person to commit a morally good act.*

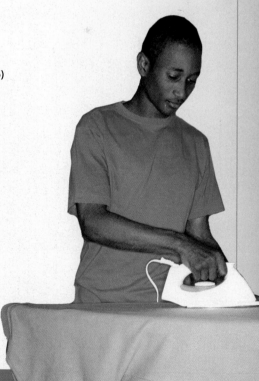

## WITH MY FAMILY

Discuss this statement as a family: It is just as important for us to be lights to one another in our family as it is for us to be lights to others in the world outside our home.

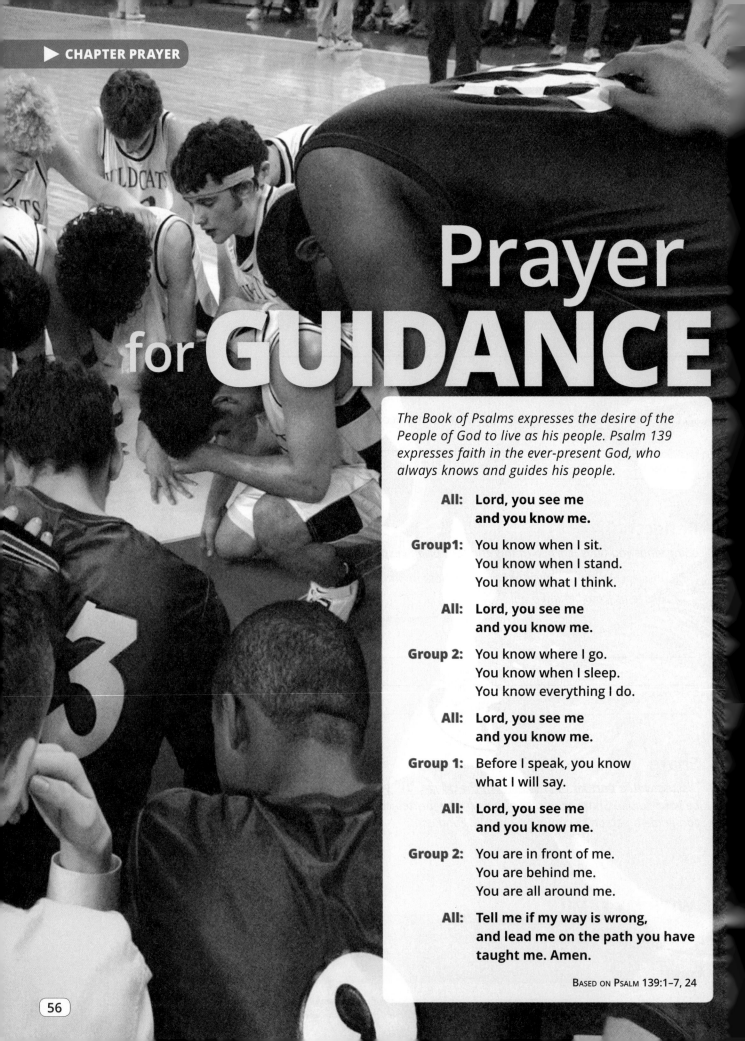

# Prayer for GUIDANCE

*The Book of Psalms expresses the desire of the People of God to live as his people. Psalm 139 expresses faith in the ever-present God, who always knows and guides his people.*

**All:** **Lord, you see me and you know me.**

**Group 1:** You know when I sit.
You know when I stand.
You know what I think.

**All:** **Lord, you see me and you know me.**

**Group 2:** You know where I go.
You know when I sleep.
You know everything I do.

**All:** **Lord, you see me and you know me.**

**Group 1:** Before I speak, you know what I will say.

**All:** **Lord, you see me and you know me.**

**Group 2:** You are in front of me.
You are behind me.
You are all around me.

**All:** **Tell me if my way is wrong, and lead me on the path you have taught me. Amen.**

BASED ON PSALM 139:1–7, 24

LOOKING AHEAD

In this chapter the Holy Spirit invites you to ▶

**EXPLORE** how two Saints exercised virtues.

**DISCOVER** the impact of different kinds of virtues.

**DECIDE** on how you can exercise virtues.

CHAPTER **5**

# The Exercise of VIRTUE

▶ When have you practiced doing little things better so you could achieve a bigger goal?

For athletes, practice makes perfect; that is striving for that "perfect" game. This is the noble cause they strive for, and is often a struggle to achieve. This is true for Christians. We too "struggle through" in practicing virtuous habits:

*For the fruit of noble struggles is a glorious one;*
*and unfailing is the root of understanding.*

WISDOM 3:15

▶ What is a good habit that you have that has helped you make good decisions?

**c380**
Saint Ambrose of Milan is first to use "cardinal virtues" in his commentary on the Gospel of Luke.

**1591–1660**
Life of Saint Louise de Marillac

| C300 | 1550 | 1650 | 1750 |

**TIMELINE**

**1553–1615**
Life of Margaret of Valois, Queen of France

**1776**
US Declaration of Independence is adopted.

# LOVE Made Visible

**S**aint Vincent de Paul is well known for his service to the poor. But his celebrity status is not what you might think. Vincent was born in 1580 into a poor family in France, and the religious life was often seen as an escape from extreme poverty. He was entrusted to the Franciscans as a teenager and ordained a priest at the age of nineteen.

After his ordination, Vincent took on responsibilities that catapulted him out of poverty. He became a chaplain to Margaret of Valois, Queen of France. He was also introduced to some of the wealthiest families in Paris. Vincent was bright with a charming personality and easily made his way into the highest segments of society. He became the personal chaplain and tutor to the Gondis family, one of the wealthiest in Paris. Vincent could have easily enjoyed a life of leisure, but God had other plans for him.

## Devoted to the Poor

On one occasion, Vincent heard the confession of a poor peasant in the Gondi estate. During this, his heart was so moved by God's grace that Vincent realized the true power of the priesthood and felt drawn to serving the poor. He desired so much to show the world the love of God. In order to do so, Vincent began a missionary group of priests devoted to working with the poor in the countryside of France. This congregation would later become known as the Vincentians.

Monsieur Vincent, as he became known, was inexhaustible in his energy and concerns. He even ministered to the galley slaves on ships. He began hospitals and orphanages. He used his contacts with the wealthy to support his endeavors. Vincent convinced a number of women in the highest realms of society to aid him in his work. They devoted themselves to the poorest of the poor in the streets of Paris.

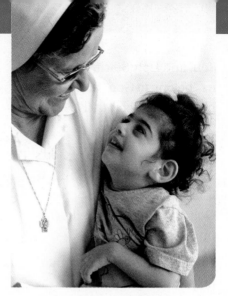

## Daughters of Charity

Also in France during this time was a woman named Louise de Marillac. She stood out for her devotion and spirituality. She had been married to a very wealthy man in Paris. After his death, Louise decided to devote her life to serving the Church by helping those people who were very poor. When she met Monsieur Vincent, she knew her prayers for serving the Church were answered.

With Vincent's help, Louise formed the Daughters of Charity. She led her new community to be in solidarity with the poor. The Daughters of Charity chose to wear gray habits with white headdresses. This was the same kind of clothing worn by poor women.

Their work spread rapidly throughout France and all of Europe. The Daughters of Charity served in hospitals, orphanages, schools, and in the homes of the poor. Louise cared for the victims of the plague during an epidemic in Paris.

## The Hard Work of Love

Both Louise and Vincent made God's love visible. They demonstrated a deep awareness of the fullness of love, as a reflection of God's love for all of us. Love for them was not some sentimental feeling. They modeled love through hard work in service to others.

Vincent wrote, "We must love God, but let it be in the work of our bodies, in the sweat of our brows." Louise reminded her sisters to "love the poor, to honor them, as you would honor Christ himself." Today the Church honors both Vincent and Louise as canonized Saints.

The loving work of Saint Vincent and Saint Louise continues today. The Daughters of Charity continue to serve the poor throughout the world. Nearly 20,000 religious women continue to serve the neediest in over ninety countries. In 1833, Frederic Ozanam formed a group of young men devoted to serving the poor in France who would eventually become known as the St. Vincent de Paul Society. Both groups continue to exercise virtuous living through acts of charity.

## Disciple POWER

### CHARITY

Love, or charity, is the Theological Virtue that draws our hearts to God because he is the source of all that is good. Love for God and love for people are inseparable. Charity seeks what is best for those we love.

## FAITH JOURNAL

How can you make love visible during difficult situations?

▶ FAITH FOCUS

How does the practice of the virtues help us grow in living the Great Commandment?

▶ FAITH VOCABULARY

Cardinal Virtues

common good

Theological Virtues

## Stay the Course

Living the Christian life means that we must practice what Jesus taught. We need to develop good habits. These habits become engrained in us and become virtues. A virtue is a habitual and firm disposition to do the good. Virtues build healthy relationships both with God and with other people. Virtues help us to do what is right and avoid what is wrong. They strengthen us to live the new life in Christ that we received in Baptism. Through virtuous living, we stay on the right course to eternal life.

▶ How do you know that you are on the "right track" with God?

## Theological Virtues

The Church teaches that there are three **Theological Virtues** and four **Cardinal Virtues**. The Theological Virtues are faith, hope, and charity, or love. The word *theological* here means "belonging to God." Theological Virtues are the strengths or habits that God gives us to help us attain holiness. They link us more closely with God the Father, Son, and Holy Spirit. They help us "belong to God" and are the pillars on which our lives in Christ are built.

**Faith.** Faith is the gift of God's invitation to believe in him. It is also the ability and power God gives us to respond to his invitation.

**Hope.** Hope is the virtue that helps us keep our focus on the Kingdom of Heaven. It enables us to trust in God and in his promises above all else.

**Charity.** Love is the good habit that helps us to put God above all else. Charity enables us to love God simply because he is God. This kind of love comes from God, and is unconditional. Charity seeks what is best for others and ourselves because God loves us. Love is the greatest of all the virtues. Saint Paul wrote,

*So faith, hope, love remain, these three; but the greatest of these is love.*

1 CORINTHIANS 13:13

▶ Who has been a role model of faith, hope and love for you?

Practicing
# Good Habits

King Solomon
(Prudence)

Moses
(Justice)

Samson
(Fortitude)

Jeremiah
(Temperance)

## Cardinal Virtues

Prudence, justice, fortitude, and temperance are the four Moral Virtues called Cardinal Virtues. The word *cardinal* comes from a Latin word meaning "hinge." Our moral life and our good moral decisions hinge on the development and practice of these four Cardinal Virtues:

- Prudence is practical wisdom, or the ability to understand what is the right response in a given situation.

- Justice is the good habit by which one truly desires what is due to others according to fundamental rights.

- Fortitude is courage, or the ability to live by our principles and values, even in the face of difficulties or danger.

- Temperance is the self-discipline needed to moderate or keep things in life balanced. Resisting indulging ourselves or controling excessive desires is a sign of a temperate person.

The more we develop the Cardinal Virtues, the better able we will be to make the good decisions to live as children of God and disciples of Jesus. And the more we cooperate with the Holy Spirit, the more we develop these virtues.

## Faith CONNECTION

Give an example of having practiced one of the Cardinal Virtues in your life.

_____

_____

_____

_____

_____

## Live Like God

Exercising virtues gives expression to those human values which best reflect the divine life. When we live virtuously, we are living like God. We live with love, mercy, integrity, compassion, responsibility, and so on. Living the virtues includes making deliberate and informed decisions. The virtues also guide us in directing our emotions for good, This means exercising the virtues enables us to live as children of God and followers of Christ.

God created us in his image and likeness. He created us to live together in a way that resembles the Holy Trinity. God is the community of perfect love. In his image, we too are to be a community of loving persons. This means that we are social creatures who need one another to be loved and to love.

## The Common Good

Society is a special form of community. A society is a group of people distinct from other groups, sharing a common culture, interests, and/or common activities. A society is made up of many types of smaller communities, such as families, schools, parishes, workplaces, towns, cities, and nations.

As Catholics, we are called to be active members of society who seek the **common good**. We cannot live only for our own self-interests, but we must seek the well-being of all peoples.

Striving to live the Great Commandment in the communities we belong to, both as individuals and as a society, is what life is all about (see Matthew 22:36–39). Achieving this goal is the common good of all members of society.

▶ What can you do to contribute to the common good?

U.S. Supreme Court Building, South Wall Frieze (left to right: Menes, Hammurabi, Moses, Authority, Solomon)

## DID YOU KNOW?

The Church encourages us to practice the Corporal Works of Mercy in order to help support the common good. These virtuous works are: feed the hungry, give drink to the thirsty, clothe the naked, shelter the homeless, visit the sick, visit the imprisoned, and bury the dead.

## Civil Authority

Public authority is exercised through the form of government often referred to as the State. The government may be at the local level, like a city council, or even in the broadest sense for a given nation, at the federal level. Civil authority has the responsibility and obligation to help individuals and the smaller communities work together for the common good. All authority, including civil authority, flows from God. Authority that exercises its power justly in society supports all the members of society to live their lives according to God's plan of creation.

Authentic civil authority maintains good order by seeking what is good for all people. True authority creates the conditions for its members to achieve the common good by creating and enforcing just, moral, and equitable laws.

True authority inspires individuals to respect others. It serves the basic human needs for life, liberty, and the pursuit of happiness. True authority protects the freedom of its members to pursue living the Great Commandment of love according to one's conscience. It creates the conditions that enable people to live the virtues and build their lives on values that reflect God's plan of creation.

▶ What are some examples of the improper use of public authority?

## Faith CONNECTION

In small groups, write a list of the top five ways in which the community of your classroom can work together for the common good. Make sure your list takes into account all members of society.

## Social Sin

Every society has the responsibility to create the conditions that enable people to live together in peace through justice. When public authority and citizens work together for the common good—when they keep in mind the well-being of one another—everyone benefits. When individuals cooperate with one another to work against human life and human rights, they sin. We call this type of sin *social sin*. We take part in social sin when we:

- participate directly and freely in another person's sin.

- order, advise, praise, or approve of another person's wrongdoing.

- fail to appropriately disclose or hinder another person's sin when we have an opportunity to do so.

- defend or protect those who commit evil acts.

## A Just Society

A society that truly works at achieving the common good is a just society. The word *just* is defined in these ways: (1) honorable and fair, (2) morally right, righteous, (3) properly due or deserved, (4) based on good reason, well-founded, and (5) lawful.

A just society is first and foremost a morally good society. It is a society that guides and supports all members to live in a right relationship with God and others. The Church's social teachings guide us in building a just society.

Christians look to Jesus and the Church for their inspiration and vision. The Church teaches us social principles for building a just society. When we work together to build a just society according to the teachings of Jesus, we are preparing the way for the coming of the Kingdom of God.

## Faith CONNECTION

**What are some of the things you see people doing to build a just society?**

# A PEOPLE of VIRTUE

**There is an old expression that says "Virtue is its own reward."** Exercising virtues will do something far better than looking good, being smart or athletically built. Virtuous living is living like God.

You will be able to look in the mirror and respect the person looking back at you. God calls all of us to be a people of virtue. Those who live the virtuous life in imitation of Christ are promised the reward of eternal life. This is part of God's plan of Salvation.

# PRACTICING VIRTUES

**Prudence.** Prudence helps you choose what is good and choose the things necessary to do what is right. You are prudent if you:

■ set aside time to do your homework first instead of putting it off until late in the night.

■ look for new friends who share your values or beliefs if the friends you have are always getting into trouble.

■ seek the help or advice of a wise and trusted adult when you find yourself in a difficult situation.

**Justice.** Justice respects the rights of every person to receive a due share in the blessings and goodness God has given to the world. You can practice justice by:

■ treating people with respect and following just rules.

■ not being prejudiced because of age, gender, ethnicity, religion, or economic status.

■ doing your best work in all that you do, at school and at home.

**Fortitude.** Fortitude is the strength and courage to do what is right and good, even when it is difficult. You practice fortitude when you:

■ stand up for Christian values when it is difficult to do so.

■ overcome obstacles and give whatever you are doing your best effort.

**Temperance.** Temperance is the attitude and habit that helps you exercise self-control. You are a temperate person when you practice self-control and discipline in whatever you are doing, even if no one is looking.

# PRACTICE MAKES PERFECT

**When you intentionally practice a good habit** or a positive attitude, it becomes easier for you to do that act or have that attitude. Eventually, it becomes a part of you. This is what is meant by a firm disposition. Developing the four Cardinal Virtues of prudence, justice, fortitude, and temperance in your daily life can help you choose to be a happy person with a truly rewarding life.

# INFLUENCES **IN LIFE**

**Reflect on the impact entertainment has on your life. How can you exercise virtues in light of such influence in your life? Who are some good role models? Explain how they live virtuous lives and imagine these are the people who deserve the "red carpet" treatment.**

_____

_____

## MY FAITH CHOICE

This week I will practice the virtues by _____

_____

_____.

**PRAY** Lord, help me to follow your ways, always being mindful of the good habits you expect of me. Amen.

## Recall

*Define each of these faith terms:*

**1.** Cardinal Virtues _____

**2.** civil authority _____

**3.** common good _____

**4.** Theological Virtues _____

**5.** social sin _____

*Choose one of the following questions and write a short answer. Share with a partner.*

**6.** What are the Theological Virtues and how do they help us live as active members of the Church?

_____

**7.** How does exercising the Cardinal Virtues keep us happy and holy?

_____

## To Help You REMEMBER

**1.** Virtues are moral habits of the will, which become a part of us.

**2.** There are three Theological Virtues and four Cardinal Virtues.

**3.** As Christians we are called to seek the common good in society for the sake of the kingdom.

## Reflect

*Using what you have learned in this chapter, briefly explain this statement:*

*Much will be required of the person entrusted with much, and still more will be demanded of the person entrusted with more.*

LUKE 12:48

_____

_____

_____

_____

## Share

*With a partner describe the common good and a just society, and explain how they are related.*

## WITH MY FAMILY

As a family, choose one of the virtues each week, and discuss how members of the family can grow in that virtue.

# Prayer for the
# EASTER VIRTUES

*Place yourself in the presence of the Lord. Close your eyes and meditate on the events of the last days of Jesus' life on Earth, one at a time. Open your eyes and quietly pray this prayer in your heart.*

Lord Jesus,

Your Resurrection
has given me
new life and
renewed hope.

Grant me
the wisdom
to know what I must do,

the will
to want to do it,

the courage
to undertake it,

the perseverance
to continue to do it,

and the strength
to complete it.

Amen.

**LOOKING AHEAD**
In this chapter the Holy Spirit invites you to ▶

**EXPLORE** the dynamic presence of the Holy Spirit.
**DISCOVER** how the Holy Spirit helps us make decisions.
**DECIDE** how you can cooperate with the Holy Spirit.

CHAPTER **6**

# The GRACE of the Holy Spirit

▶ Which talents has God given you? How have you used or not used them?

Saint Paul often opened and closed his letters by invoking God's presence or blessing. Here is an example:

*Grace to you and peace from God our Father and the Lord Jesus Christ.*

PHILEMON 1:3

▶ How does keeping God at the forefront of our lives help us make good decisions?

**TIMELINE**

| | | | |
|---|---|---|---|
| **1881** Fr. Michael J. McGivney forms the Knights of Columbus. | | **1963** Vatican II restores the use of the RCIA. | **1997** *Catechism of the Catholic Church* is promulgated. |

1840 — 1880 — 1920 — 1960 — 2000

**1854** US PTO distribute seed varieties.

**1980** SCOTUS rules in *Diamond v Chakrabarty*.

# A Spirit-filled PEOPLE

**O**ne of the best places to look for the grace of the Holy Spirit is in the life of a local parish. St. Bridget Catholic Church is a large suburban parish. There are seven Masses celebrated on the weekend. Four are celebrated in English, one in Spanish, one in Italian and one in Vietnamese. A quick glance at the weekly bulletin gives a sense of how diverse, alive and Spirit-filled this community is.

## Diverse Gifts

The parish's calendar is jam-packed each and every week. The diverse gifts of this parish are on display every week. This upcoming week is no different:

- Sunday afternoon, eleven babies will be baptized!

- Sunday evening there is the youth ministry's weekly meeting. They are planning a fundraiser to sponsor a "mission possible" spring break mission trip for people living on the Texas-Mexico border just outside of Matamoros, Mexico.

- On Monday night, there is an RCIA meeting for adults preparing for their baptism at the Easter Vigil. Twelve adults, their godparents and two catechists are exploring the meaning of the Eucharist on this night.

- Tuesday evenings, there is a Knights of Columbus meeting in the church basement.

- On Thursday nights, two hundred eighth graders will show up for their sacramental preparation classes. On this night there is a special guest speaker talking about the meaning of Confirmation.

- Throughout the day on Fridays, the parish food pantry helps families in need by giving them bags of groceries.

▶ How involved are you in your parish youth group?

## Committed to the Community

Throughout the week and scattered throughout the community, several parishioners are committing themselves to serving those in need. They are visiting home-bound senior citizens, some bringing food, others company, still others the Eucharist.

The parish is also involved in an interfaith homeless project. More than thirty men and several women come to a community shelter where they are given a hot meal, a place to sleep, breakfast in the morning and a bagged lunch.

And almost every weekday evening, the religious education program is active, with sixth through eighth graders meeting on Wednesday nights.

Then there is the Pro-Life Committee who is sponsoring a series of talks for the diocese. The series is titled: "The Gospel of Life."

▶ What do you know about the "gospel of life"?

## Symphony of Faith

The parish also supports various groups who help with the internal needs of the parish. These needs include parishioners dealing with grief, divorce, unemployment or severe health concerns.

These are just some of the day-in and day-out events in the spirit-filled life of St. Bridget Catholic Church. Such committed people like those at St. Bridget give evidence to the grace of the Holy Spirit at work. Through such diverse individuals with many different gifts, the Spirit animates the Church.

The pastor of the parish describes his job as the conductor of this great symphony of faith. He tries to make sure that the Spirit of God is given free reign to work through these wonderfully committed people. This is all about real people with real faith being led by the Holy Spirit.

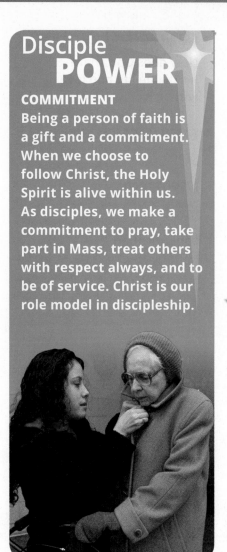

## Disciple POWER

### COMMITMENT

Being a person of faith is a gift and a commitment. When we choose to follow Christ, the Holy Spirit is alive within us. As disciples, we make a commitment to pray, take part in Mass, treat others with respect always, and to be of service. Christ is our role model in discipleship.

## FAITH JOURNAL

How do you demonstrate your commitment to live out your faith?

▶ **FAITH FOCUS**

How does God share his divine life and love with us?

▶ **FAITH VOCABULARY**

grace

justification

merit

sanctification

# Seeking
# New LIFE

## Sowing Grace

Jesus taught that the Spirit works in us through **grace**. He taught us how grace can grow within us. Grace is like a seed that God freely plants within us. The parable of the Sower can help us understand the role of grace in our lives.

*A very large crowd gathered around [Jesus] so that he got into a boat on the sea and sat down. And the whole crowd was beside the sea on land. And he taught them at length in parables, and in the course of his instruction he said to them, "Hear this! A sower went out to sow. And as he sowed, some seed fell on the path, and the birds came and ate it up. Other seed fell on rocky ground where it had little soil. It sprang up at once because the soil was not deep. And when the sun rose, it was scorched and it withered for lack of roots. Some seed fell among thorns, and the thorns grew up and choked it and it produced no grain. And some seed fell on rich soil and produced fruit. It came up and grew and yielded thirty, sixty, and a hundredfold."* Mark 4:1–8

When he was alone with his disciples, Jesus helped them understand the meaning of the parable. He explained that the seed that fell on the path and

*The Sower* by Vincent Van Gogh, oil on canvas, 1888.

rocky ground and among the thorns either died or did not bear much fruit. He then explained,

*"But those sown on rich soil are the ones who hear the word and accept it and bear fruit thirty and sixty and a hundredfold."*

MARK 4:20

In this parable, God is like the sower of the seed. Out of his unlimited generosity, he sows his loving grace everywhere. God plants the seeds of faith, hope, and love in our hearts because of his love for us. God prepares the soil, plants the seeds, and provides the proper nutrients to ensure a bountiful crop. This is how grace nurtures our faith, and enables us to make good moral decisions.

▶ **When have you experienced the seeds of grace bearing fruit in your life?**

## Stewards of Grace

While God does sow the seeds of grace in our lives, it does not mean that all we do is sit back and let God tend the seeds he has planted within us. If that is our attitude, God's grace and his Word will not bear much fruit in our lives. The life of grace within us can wither or be choked up and produce nothing. Our participation makes all the difference.

▶ **How do you know your participation in grace makes a difference?**

Grace enables us to participate in the very life of God, a sharing in the intimacy enjoyed by the Father, Son, and Holy Spirit. This grace is the free and undeserved gift by which we are united with God. His grace empowers us to love him who first loved us.

When unimpeded by our sins and when nurtured by faith, prayer, and the Sacraments, grace produces life in abundance for us. Jesus said that we will even share in the divine life "thirty, sixty, and a hundredfold" (Mark 4:8). These seeds of grace sown by God in our lives have the potential to yield a spectacular harvest. And each of us is expected to be a good steward of that grace.

God's love for us is so great that without taking away our freedom he responds to the deepest desire of our hearts to share in his life. God not only places this desire within us, but strengthens us so that our search for that happiness can be successful. In other words, that bountiful harvest of faith, hope, and love is made fruitful in his grace.

## Sharing in God's Life

The first eight chapters of the Book of Genesis are a brilliant description of God's plan for humanity. Genesis begins with a creation story which emphasizes that God created human beings in his image and likeness. Since God is a community of love, man is not meant to be alone. The man Adam and the woman Eve are made for each other and complete each other.

Yet the harmony between God and the first humans was eventually broken by sin. Adam and Eve are banished from Eden and must find their way in the world through hard work and labor pains. Things go from bad to worse as Cain kills his brother, Abel, and the world becomes engulfed in sin. The Genesis story describes the fallen human condition.

Yet God does not give up on humanity. Instead, he forms a covenant with his chosen people. The Covenant and God's Law offer all of us a way through the darkness of sin.

The Covenant is fulfilled in Jesus Christ, the Son of God. In Christ, God offers himself as a perfect sacrifice for our Redemption. Through Jesus, God asks for us to live in faith, hope and love. This intimacy with God is grace. Paul describes it this way:

> *For those who are led by the Spirit of God are children of God. For you did not receive a spirit of slavery to fall back into fear, but you received a spirit of adoption, through which we cry out "Abba, Father!"*
>
> ROMANS 8:14-15

The Father sent his Son so that we may participate in the divine life. The Risen Christ lives on in the Church through the power of Holy Spirit. Through Baptism, we receive the gift of sanctifying grace that makes us sharers in God's life. Infused by the Holy Spirit at Baptism, sanctifying grace is the love of God entering our souls, healing us from sin, and restoring our holiness. This life of holiness is our sharing in the life of God the Father, Son, and Holy Spirit.

▶ How is receiving a sacrament, such as Holy Communion, an intimate experience of grace for you?

## In Right Relations

In Christ, God has restored the human condition according to his plan. In Christ, we are given God's grace, and we learn what it really means to be human. Jesus, in his humanity, is the new Adam. Jesus shows us how we can be faithful to God.

Jesus is both divine and human. He offers us a sharing in his divine life. The new life offered to us is called **justification**. We have been reconciled to God in Christ. We are set in right relationship with God. What Adam and Eve lost, Jesus has restored! As Paul describes, Jesus is "a life-giving spirit" (1 Corinthians 15:45).

▶ How is the spirit of Jesus a reality in your life?

## Made Holy

After Jesus ascended to Heaven, the Father sent the Holy Spirit to accompany us down life's twisting paths. By the indwelling presence of the Holy Spirit, we are made holy. "Uniting us by faith and Baptism to the Passion and Resurrection of Christ, the Spirit makes us sharers in his life" (*Catechism of the Catholic Church* 2017).

This work of the Holy Spirit is called **sanctification**. We can accept forgiveness and the gift of having our friendships with God restored. We can grow in our abilities to make right choices and live as God's adopted children. Our justification, our Salvation in Christ, is the work of God's loving mercy. Justification has as its goal the glory of God, and the gift of our eternal life with him.

## Faith CONNECTION

Within a small group offer evidence that the Holy Spirit is at work in the world around you. Cite specific examples and explain your reasons.

## Faith CONNECTION

Think of someone who has made a difference by cooperating with the grace of the Holy Spirit. Design a "merit badge" with a motto to honor this person.

## A Share in Grace

Jesus tells a parable about an official who owed a huge debt to a king (see Matthew 18:21–35). When the official begged for mercy, the king forgave his whole debt.

The official in the Gospel parable did not **merit** the king's mercy. The word merit means "to be worthy of, deserve." Something we merit is something that we are entitled to or worthy of. It is a reward that we have earned because of certain tasks we have successfully accomplished.

For example, students merit good grades because they study hard and successfully pass a course or test.

God owes us nothing. Every blessing, every grace we have received, God freely gives us out of his love for us. How then can we talk about meriting God's free gifts of mercy, forgiveness, and Salvation? No one can merit the initial grace that calls us back to God. We can only merit grace because God has chosen to allow us to share in his work of grace.

## Source of Merit

Cooperating with the Holy Spirit, we can merit certain blessings and graces needed for living our lives as children of God here on Earth and for attaining eternal life in Heaven. Cooperating with the Holy Spirit, we first seek the Kingdom of God. Then all things will be given to us (read Matthew 6:33).

Jesus' love is the source of all merit before God. God gives us his grace through his Son, whose love has won us everything. Jesus is the key to understanding the concepts of grace, justification, and merit. Meriting eternal life is first of all associated with the grace of God and, second, with our cooperation. By cooperating with the Holy Spirit, we merit the rewards God has prepared for us.

# Responding in LOVE

**In this chapter,** you learned about the grace of the Holy Spirit and how grace is active in our lives. Through prayer and the grace of the Holy Spirit, we are able to remain open and respond to God's goodness in ourselves and others.

As a follower of Jesus, you are asked to see God in all those whom you meet. We are all God's children and he dwells within every one of us. People from all different cultures—people who seem just like us and people who seem very different—are all children of God.

## WITH DIGNITY **AND RESPECT**

**God created and loves each and every person.** The grace of the Holy Spirit enables you to respect the uniqueness of each person. Jesus spent a lot of time teaching about love and living the commandment to love. You are to love others—without exception—just as Jesus did and commanded all of his disciples to do. Your response of love is an acknowledgment that every person is created and loved by God. Your responsibility is to treat every person with dignity and respect.

# MAKE A DIFFERENCE

**When people are not willing** to accept the responsibility of treating others with dignity and respect, the results can be horrendous. You have heard and read about violence, abuse, and crimes. You can, instead, work to build attitudes that lead to love. You can make a difference by:

- remembering that God dwells in each person. Say to yourself whenever you see others, "The Lord is them." When you can make this a habit, you will find it easier to respect others.

- looking for the goodness in others. God is not finished with any of us yet. We can all grow and change and become better people.

- affirming the positive qualities and characteristics of others and supporting them in the use of their gifts and talents.

- doing random acts of kindness because you believe that people are worth it.

# DO UNTO **OTHERS**

**Work in small groups.** Imagine that you have been hired as the writers for a new TV series called "Do Unto Others." Each week the show will present a dilemma that is solved by people choosing to respect one another. Make up titles for the first three episodes.

- Choose one of the titles and outline the screenplay. Share your outline with the other groups.

## MY FAITH CHOICE

This week I will show that I believe all people have dignity. I will: _____

_____ .

 **PRAY**  Holy Spirit, help guide me in my thoughts and actions this week. Help me to accept others and see your spirit alive in them. Amen.

## Recall

*Define each of these faith terms:*

**1.** grace _____

**2.** sanctification _____

**3.** justification _____

**4.** merit _____

*Choose one of the following questions, and write a short answer. Share with a partner.*

**5.** Discuss the importance of freely responding to God's grace.

_____

_____

**6.** Discuss how grace is different than law.

_____

_____

**7.** Explain the role of the Holy Spirit in the life of grace.

_____

_____

## To Help You REMEMBER

**1.** Grace is the very life of God within us, and our participation in his plan.

**2.** Justification is the new life of grace offered to us in Christ.

**3.** The Holy Spirit offers the gift of sanctification, a sharing in the holiness of God.

## Reflect

*Using what you have learned in this chapter, briefly explain this statement:*

*Seek first the kingdom [of God] and his righteousness, and all these things will be given you besides.*

MATTHEW 6:33

_____

_____

## Share

*Describe to a partner how the parable of the Sower helps you better understand grace.*

## WITH MY FAMILY

As a family, discuss how your family shows that you all are cooperating with God's gift of grace to live as a Christian family.

# Prayer
to the
# HOLY SPIRIT

**All:** In the name of the Father, and of the Son, and of the Holy Spirit. Amen.

**Leader:** Let us pray to the Holy Spirit for the grace to live as faithful followers of Jesus.

Come, Holy Spirit, fill the hearts of your faithful and kindle in them the fire of your love.

**Group 1:** Help us honor all people as children of God and treat them with respect.

**All:** Holy Spirit, kindle in us the fire of your love.

**Group 2:** Open our hearts to your grace that we may treat others with kindness and generosity.

**All:** Holy Spirit, kindle in us the fire of your love.

**Group 3:** Teach us to work for peace and justice and to bring comfort to those who are suffering.

**All:** Holy Spirit, kindle in us the fire of your love.

**Leader:** God, our Father, send the Holy Spirit, to guide and teach us, to renew the faith of the Earth by living as your Son taught us. We ask this in his name.

**All:** Amen.

NAME _____

## Ⓐ Choose the Best Word

*Answer each question by circling the best answer.*

**1.** What is the mission of the Church given to her by Jesus?

    A. being witnesses for Christ

    B. making disciples of all nations

    C. sharing God's love with everyone

    D. all of the above

**2.** What is Christian morality?

    A. the Passion, Death, and Resurrection of Christ

    B. the way of living our lives as disciples of Jesus according to Church teachings

    C. the way of life for a group of teenagers

    D. the root of all morality

**3.** What is conscience?

    A. a little man inside our heads

    B. a persistent voice that helps us make good moral choices

    C. the Holy Spirit

    D. our soul

**4.** What are the Cardinal Virtues?

    A. prudence, love, justice, and temperance

    B. hope, charity, justice, and peace

    C. prudence, justice, fortitude, and temperance

    D. prudence, hope, charity, and peace

**5.** What does the goodness or evil of an act depend on?

    A. morality, virtues, and actions

    B. object, intention, and circumstances

    C. intentions, actions, and emotions

    D. none of the above

## B  Show What You Know

*Match the item in Column A with those in Column B.*

**Column A**

_____ 1. evangelization

_____ 2. sanctifying grace

_____ 3. actual grace

_____ 4. justification

_____ 5. dignity

_____ 6. soul

_____ 7. Theological Virtues

_____ 8. free will

_____ 9. Paschal Mystery

_____ 10. mortal sin

**Column B**

**A.** our personal participation in the life of the Trinity

**B.** divine help empowering us to live as children of God

**C.** the proclamation of the Gospel

**D.** deadly sin

**E.** faith, hope, and charity

**F.** Passion, Death, Resurrection, and glorious Ascension

**G.** the worthiness that comes from being created in God's image

**H.** making things right through Christ

**I.** the immortal part of a person

**J.** the power to choose between good and evil

## C  Connect with Scripture

*Reread the Scripture passage on the first Unit Opener page.
What connection do you see between this passage and what you
learned in this unit?*

_____

_____

_____

## D  Be a Disciple

**1.** *Review The Church Follows Jesus in each of the chapters. Which
person or ministry of the Church has inspired you to be a better
disciple of Jesus? Explain your response.*

_____

_____

_____

**2.** *Work with a group. Review the six Disciple Power habits you have
learned about in this unit. After jotting down your own ideas, share
with the group practical ways that you will live these day by day.*

_____

_____

_____

# The WAY to MORAL LIVING

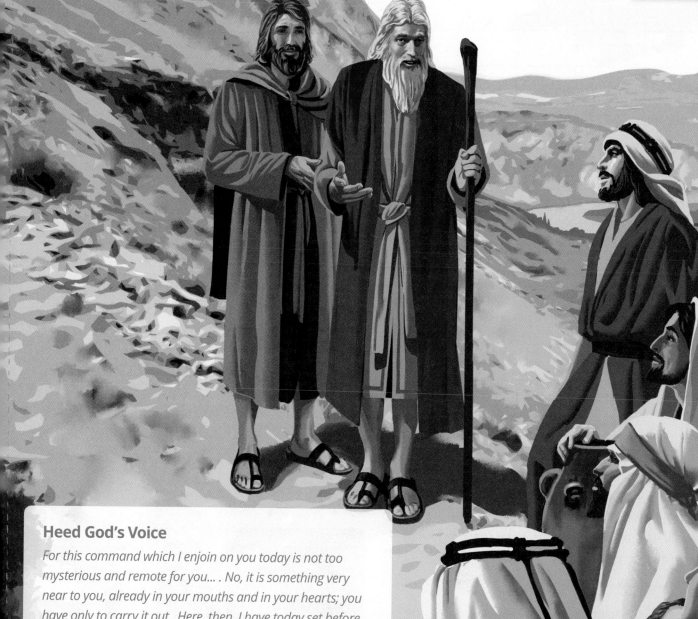

## Heed God's Voice

*For this command which I enjoin on you today is not too mysterious and remote for you... . No, it is something very near to you, already in your mouths and in your hearts; you have only to carry it out . Here, then, I have today set before you life and prosperity, death and doom . If you obey the commandments of the Lord, your God, which I enjoin on you today, loving him, and walking in his ways, and keeping his commandments, statutes and decrees, you will live and grow numerous, and the Lord, your God, will bless you in the land you are entering to occupy. If, however, you turn away your hearts and will not listen, but are led a stray and adore and serve other gods, I tell you now that you will certainly perish. . . . I have set before you life and death, the blessing and the curse. Choose life, then, that you and your descendants may live, by loving the Lord, your God, heeding his voice, and holding fast to him .*                                   Deuteronomy 30: 11, 14-20a

## What I Already Know

*Complete the following sentences.*

The Beatitudes are . . .

_____

_____

_____

The precepts of the Church are . . .

_____

_____

_____

Grace is . . .

_____

_____

_____

## Faith Vocabulary

*With a partner, take turns choosing words and defining them for each other. If there are words that neither of you can define, put a check mark next to them.*

_____ laity

_____ conscience

_____ integrity

_____ blasphemy

_____ justice

_____ euthanasia

_____ fidelity

_____ chastity

## What I Want to Know

*Write a question you have under each heading.*

**Sacred Scripture**
*What would you like to know about free will?*

_____

_____

_____

**The Church**
*What would you like to know about the Church's authority?*

_____

_____

_____

**Another Question I Have**

_____

_____

_____

**LOOKING AHEAD**
In this chapter the Holy Spirit invites you to ▶

**EXPLORE** the extraordinary life of Pope Saint John XXIII.
**DISCOVER** the teachings of the Second Vatican Council.
**DECIDE** how you can witness your faith in the community.

CHAPTER **7**

# A Pilgrim Church

▶ **What inspires you in life to take action?**

The Holy Spirit continually breathes new life into the Church. Such an example is when the Church raises up new leaders with new visions to meet new challenges. One such vision was the Second Vatican Council under the leadership of Pope John XXIII, who reminded us of these words from Scripture:

> . . . *I will pour out my spirit upon all mankind.*
> *Your sons and daughters shall prophesy,*
> *your old men shall dream dreams,*
> *your young men shall see visions; . . .*
>
> JOEL 3:1

▶ **How might this passage inspire the youth today?**

**TIMELINE**

| | | | |
|---|---|---|---|
| **1958–1963** Papacy of John XXIII | **1963–1978** Papacy of Paul VI | **1991** Enthronement of Ecumenical Patriarch Bartholomew | |

1950 — 1960 — 1970 — 1980 — 1990 — 2000 — 2010

**1962–1965** Second Vatican Council

**2013** Election of Jorge Mario Bergoglio as Pope

# Let Your Light Shine

**E**very human being has within them the light of faith, hope and love. The mission of every person is to let that light shine. Some people's light shines not just on their family, friends and community, but the whole world. Pope John XXIII was one of those people.

He was born Angelo Roncalli in northern Italy on November 25, 1881. He was the third of thirteen children. Perhaps this large family was part of the reason why he later became known as "the people's pope." He was a very bright man, but was best known for his warm and friendly personality. Pope John XXIII was always a person of deep faith and his hope-filled spirituality was evident by his open heart and mind.

Becoming a priest was for Angelo a natural reflection of the faith shining within him. He was quickly elevated to secretary to the bishop. Father Angelo eventually became a spiritual director, with concern for the daily life of the average person.

## Renewing the Spirit

Father Angelo Roncalli was ordained a bishop in 1925 and spent a great deal of his time in Bulgaria, Turkey and Greece. When World War II broke out, he was instrumental in helping save the lives of many Jewish families.

After the war, he was appointed Patriarch of Venice and was delighted to finally return home. Yet his time in Venice was brief. God had other plans for him.

Much to his shock, and to the surprise of the world, Bishop Roncalli was elected Pope in 1958. He chose the papal name John XXIII. He described himself as a shepherd and a priest.

Pope John XXIII quickly became well-known for his walks through the streets of Rome, and visits to the hospitals, schools and prisons in Rome. He was a man with a wise wit and humbling humor. When asked why he wanted to go visit the prisoners, the Pope said, "Because they cannot come to me." When asked how many people worked in the Vatican, he replied, "About half of them."

During this time, the world was changing and there were many Catholics who believed the Church needed to become more in touch with the modern world. Pope John XXIII called the Second Vatican Council. The purpose of this Council was *aggiornamento*—a renewal within the Church. The Pope gathered together all the Catholic bishops to discuss the future of the Church. The Second Vatican Council was an opportunity to renew the spirit of the Church and within the Church.

Pope John XXIII did not live to see the Council completed. He died in 1963, the year *Time* magazine chose him as "Man of the Year." He was a saintly man who belonged not only to the Church but to the world. At every stage of his life, Pope John XXIII exemplified the Holy Spirit's gift of wisdom. Because of his ordinary appeal, Blessed Pope John XXIII left a lasting legacy.

## FAITH JOURNAL

List one way in which you feel connected to the Pope. How has he left a lasting impression on your faith?

▶ **FAITH FOCUS**

What were some of the key teachings of Vatican II?

---

▶ **FAITH VOCABULARY**

ecumenical council

laity

solidarity

## The Church Today

Imagine that you are part of a parish youth ministry program. On Sunday evening, there is Mass with contemporary music. A band leads the music with guitars, drums and a piano. You are a lector at Mass and your older sister is an extraordinary minister of the Eucharist. On the following Tuesday, you and the rest of the youth group help set up meals and cots for a homeless project.

This scenario is not uncommon in the Catholic Church today. Many parish activities are a result from the teachings of the Second Vatican Council. This **ecumenical council** brought together all the bishops of the Church to discuss the contemporary issues facing the Church. They used Church teachings to address concerns of modern society. In this chapter, you will discover some of the Council's most important teachings that help us face today's challenges.

▶ **What are some challenges you face in your faith?**

## Growing in Faith

The Council produced many documents, all at different levels of teachings. Some teachings of the Church, like a *dogmatic constitution*, are to be given a greater acceptance in faith than a document like an *apostolic letter* from the Pope. Vatican II published two very important documents that shed new light on the Church's teachings. These documents, like all Vatican documents, are known by a Latin name based on the first few words of the document.

# Guided by the SPIRIT

The first major Vatican II document was *Dei Verbum*, a dogmatic constitution about the Word of God. The second document was called *Lumen Gentium*. This dogmatic constitution described the Church as a mystery in which God is at work. This mystery includes both the **laity** and the clergy of the Church. We are a pilgrim Church on a journey of faith, guided by the Spirit, yet always in need of greater growth.

▶ How are you in need of greater growth in your faith?

## Light of Nations

God calls the entire Church to holiness. This includes ordained ministers (bishops, priests, and deacons), consecrated religious (such as monks and nuns), and all of the laity (who are either single or married). The laity are called to live a life of deep faith and to follow Christ in all things. The laity is to share with the world the Catholic faith in Christ, who is the Light of nations.

▶ What does *lumen gentium* mean in English?

The Pope and the bishops have a teaching authority within the Church called the Magisterium.

They guide the laity in properly understanding the teachings of Jesus. Each of us is responsible for learning the teachings of the Church and to best understand and accept them as acts of faith, hope and charity. We, the laity within the Church, are to evangelize the world by the light of faith, echoing the Word of God. In this way, we witness for Christ, sharing the Gospel and aiding the hierarchical leadership of the Church to make disciples of all nations.

## Joy and Hope

The final constitution of the Second Vatican Council was *Gaudium et Spes*. This pastoral document focuses on the relationship between the Church and the modern world. The Council made it clear that the Church must be continually engaged in the world. The opening words of this document make clear that whatever humanity experiences, such as joy and hope or fear and anxiety, the Church too experiences these through the followers of Jesus (read *Gaudium et Spes* 1). The Church is to help shed light on the human condition, and participate in addressing the needs of the world.

89

## One in the World

The Catholic Church does not exist apart from the world. In fact, the Church is to be Christ in the world. That is, God calls the Church to transform the world. For the Church, the needs of our world are at the heart of her mission. This outreach attitude of the Church reflects the words of Jesus in the Gospel of John:

> For God so loved the world that he gave his only Son, so that everyone who believes in him might not perish but might have eternal life. For God did not send his Son into the world to condemn the world, but that the world might be saved through him.
>
> JOHN 3:16–17

The Church as our Mother and Teacher nurtures the faith of every child of God. She reaches out with her loving embrace to comfort those in need, helps the poor, and reconciles sinners with God and one another. This deep connection to the human race and history is called **solidarity**. The Church serves the world so that every person may experience oneness as brothers and sisters in Christ.

## Serving the World

The Church exists not only for her own member but exists to be a servant to the world. This service involves reaching out to those in need, and includes a special wisdom that can serve as a guiding light for the world. As the Council fathers wrote:

> Inspired by no earthly ambition, the Church seeks but a solitary goal: to carry forward the work of Christ under the lead of the befriending Spirit. And Christ entered this world to give witness to the truth, to rescue and not to sit in judgment, to serve and not to be served (*Gaudium et Spes* 3).

▶ How can you carry on the work of Christ in the world?

## Speaking Truth

The Second Vatican Council taught that the mission of the Church is to read the signs of the times and to interpret them in light of the Gospel. The "signs of the times" refer to the specific issues, questions, confusions, hopes, and dreams of each generation. The Church must respond to the very specific issues of the time and in the world. The Church must be attentive to the current events and be able to speak the truth, with hope and charity in the face of any challenge.

In an ever-changing world, there does remain unchanging truth. For example, Jesus Christ is Lord and Savior. Christ alone answers the deepest needs of humanity. As

the Council fathers wrote:

> The Church firmly believes that Christ, who died and was raised up for all, can through His Spirit offer man the light and the strength to measure up to his supreme destiny. Nor has any other name under the heaven been given to man by which it is fitting for him to be saved (*Gaudium et Spes* 10).

▶ How does the Church speak the truth to you?

## In God's Image

At the heart of the Church's message for humanity is Christ. In and through Christ, the Church proclaims the inherent dignity of the human person. This means that each person deserves to be treated with love and respect, just as Jesus did and taught. The true value of the human person is based on the truth that each of us is created in the image and likeness of God. God created us as social beings. We are to be a communion of persons as God the Holy Trinity is.

Though due to sin, we can be blind to the dignity of the human person, we can find hope in the truth that Christ has won Redemption for all of us. Through the grace of the Holy Spirit, we can come to know and love the goodness of God. And through the Light of God, we can find true wisdom (read *Gaudium et Spes* 13, 15).

## Faith CONNECTION

Discuss with a partner one way in which you experience a sense of oneness and dignity because of your Christian faith.

## Our Inner Sanctuary

The conscience holds a special place of honor in the dignity of the human person. The Council fathers eloquently declared that:

> "Man has in his heart a law inscribed by God. His dignity lies in observing this law, and by it he will be judged. His conscience is man's most secret core and sanctuary. There he is alone with God whose voice echoes in his depths" (*Gaudium et Spes* 16).

Through the conscience each of us is able to discern what God has determined to be good and evil. The conscience works with the will, aiding each person to intentionally choose to do what is good. When we do good, we honor human dignity.

▶ **What good actions have you done that honor human dignity?**

## Challenging the World

Reading the signs of the times means that the Church must be unafraid to proclaim the truth. Throughout her history, the Church has continually challenged the world to stand up for what is right.

During the Industrial Revolution, the Church spoke out against the unjust treatment of workers and the dangerous conditions which too many workers had to endure. During the Cold War, the Church declared the nuclear arms race to be a grave danger upon all of humanity. Post Cold War, the Church challenged nations to insure that economic systems do not place profit over people.

Today, the Church strongly defends marriage as a sacred lifelong bond between one man and one woman. She affirms the uniqueness of each gender and the importance of human sexuality as a gift from God. And the Church has consistently affirmed that human life must be protected from the moment of conception until natural death. Her pro-life stance not only encompasses protecting the unborn and the terminally ill; the Church reminds us all that everyone, including convicted criminals, have an inherent dignity that we must never violate with our actions. In every generation, the Church has been society's conscience speaking to our hearts.

## Faith CONNECTION

Create a logo or symbol that honors human dignity.

# A Faithful HEART

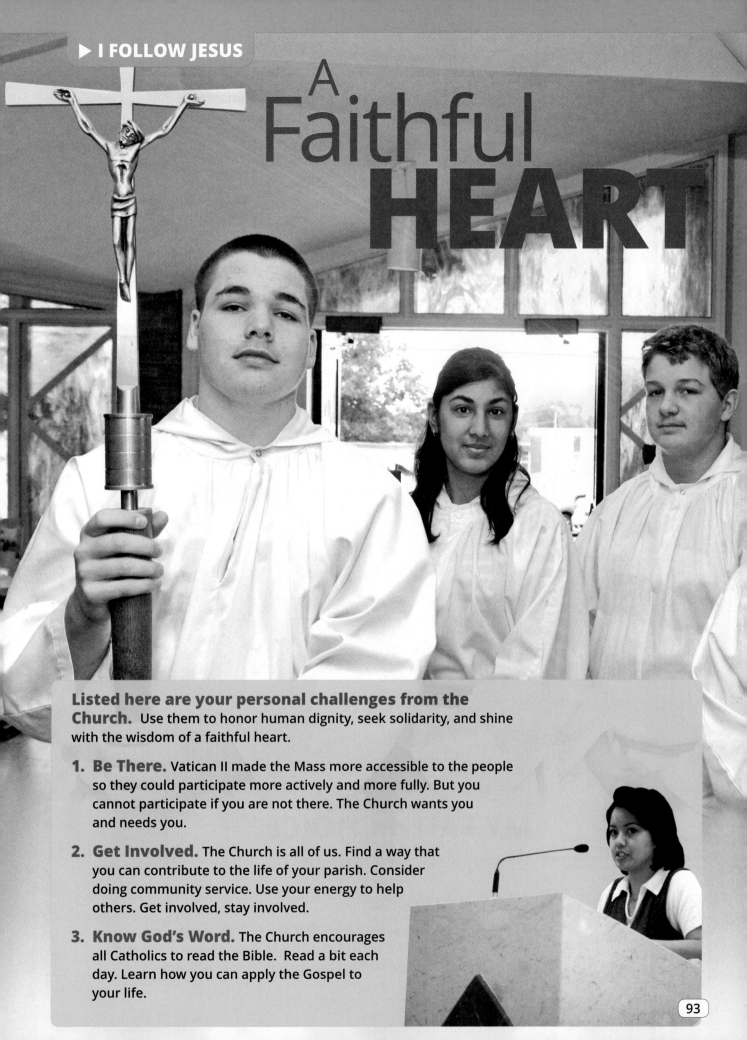

**Listed here are your personal challenges from the Church.** Use them to honor human dignity, seek solidarity, and shine with the wisdom of a faithful heart.

1. **Be There.** Vatican II made the Mass more accessible to the people so they could participate more actively and more fully. But you cannot participate if you are not there. The Church wants you and needs you.

2. **Get Involved.** The Church is all of us. Find a way that you can contribute to the life of your parish. Consider doing community service. Use your energy to help others. Get involved, stay involved.

3. **Know God's Word.** The Church encourages all Catholics to read the Bible. Read a bit each day. Learn how you can apply the Gospel to your life.

93

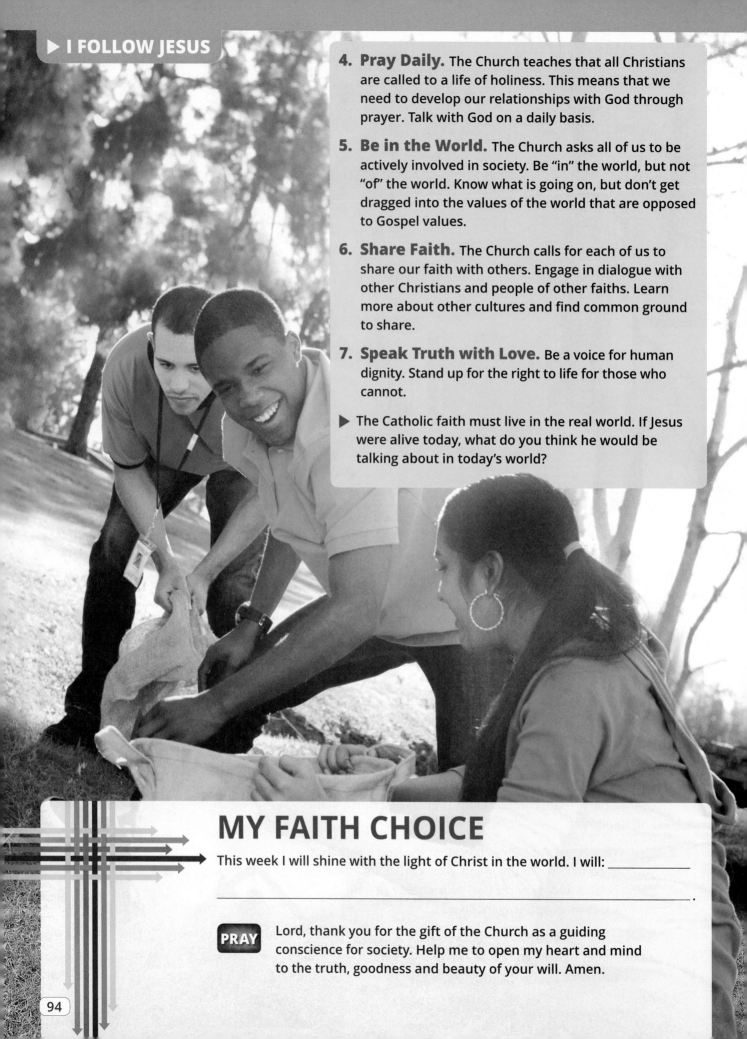

4. **Pray Daily.** The Church teaches that all Christians are called to a life of holiness. This means that we need to develop our relationships with God through prayer. Talk with God on a daily basis.

5. **Be in the World.** The Church asks all of us to be actively involved in society. Be "in" the world, but not "of" the world. Know what is going on, but don't get dragged into the values of the world that are opposed to Gospel values.

6. **Share Faith.** The Church calls for each of us to share our faith with others. Engage in dialogue with other Christians and people of other faiths. Learn more about other cultures and find common ground to share.

7. **Speak Truth with Love.** Be a voice for human dignity. Stand up for the right to life for those who cannot.

▶ The Catholic faith must live in the real world. If Jesus were alive today, what do you think he would be talking about in today's world?

# MY FAITH CHOICE

This week I will shine with the light of Christ in the world. I will: _____

_____ .

**PRAY**  Lord, thank you for the gift of the Church as a guiding conscience for society. Help me to open my heart and mind to the truth, goodness and beauty of your will. Amen.

## Recall

*Define each of these faith terms:*

**1.** ecumenical council _____

**2.** solidarity _____

**3.** laity _____

*Choose one of the following questions, and write a short answer. Share with a partner your response.*

**4.** How did Vatican II change the way we celebrate the Mass?

_____

_____

**5.** What did Vatican II teach about the Church in the world today?

_____

_____

## Reflect

*Using what you have learned in this chapter, briefly explain how this Scripture passage relates to the teachings of Vatican II:*

*"I have much more to tell you, but you cannot bear it now. But when he comes, the Spirit of truth, he will guide you to all truth."*

JOHN 16:12–13

_____

_____

_____

## Share

*Discuss with a partner the role of the Church in helping with the needs of the world.*

## WITH MY FAMILY

Spend time during the weekends working on how each family member can challenge the others to speak out in defense of human dignity.

### To Help You REMEMBER

**1.** The Second Vatican Council helped the Church respond to the needs of today's world.

**2.** The Church must read the signs of the times and interpret them in light of the Gospel.

**3.** We are called to honor the dignity of the human person as Christ did.

# Prayer of the FAITHFUL

**Leader:** Let us pray that the Holy Spirit may continue to guide the Church in all that she does and says.

**Reader 1:** We pray for the Pope and our bishop, that their faith and love may be a sign of hope to all the world.

**All:** Lord, hear our prayer.

**Reader 2:** We pray for peace in our world, especially for all of the children and families who are victims of war and violence.

**All:** Lord, hear our prayer.

**Reader 3:** We pray for those we find difficult to understand. We pray for those we find difficult to like. May we hear and see them as God does.

**All:** Lord, hear our prayer.

**Reader 4:** We pray for all who experience prejudice. We pray for those who speak hatred. May their hearts be healed and reconciled with God and others.

**All:** Lord, hear our prayer.

**Reader 5:** We pray for all who are hungry this week. May our care and compassion make a difference in their lives.

**All:** Lord, hear our prayer.

**Reader 6:** We pray for our parents, grandparents, and all who have raised us. We pray in gratitude for their loving care.

**All:** Lord, hear our prayer. Amen.

**LOOKING AHEAD**
In this chapter the Holy
Spirit invites you to ▶

**EXPLORE** the core precepts of the Church.
**DISCOVER** the meaning of the first three Commandments.
**DECIDE** to reject false idols in the world today.

CHAPTER **8**

# To Love God above All

▶ Describe an experience that was frustrating because the directions were unclear or not included.

Imagine a highway system with no road signs. You have no GPS device. You would have a difficult time getting to your destination. Similarly, the Israelites had trouble finding their destination of the Promised Land during the Exodus. Moses went up Mount Sinai, and God gave him and the Israelites the Ten Commandments to help them find their eternal destination:

> *Your word, LORD, stands forever;*
>   *it is firm as the heavens.*
> *Through all generations your truth endures;*
>   *fixed to stand firm like the earth.*        PSALM 119:89–90

▶ In what ways do the Ten Commandments give your life direction?

**TIMELINE**

590
Pope Gregory I establishes
Gregorian chant.

c.700
Pope Gregory III dedicates
Nov 1st as All Saints Day.

787
Council of Nicaea II

500        550        600        650        700        750        800        850        900

795
Vikings first raid Ireland.

c.900
First example of music notation

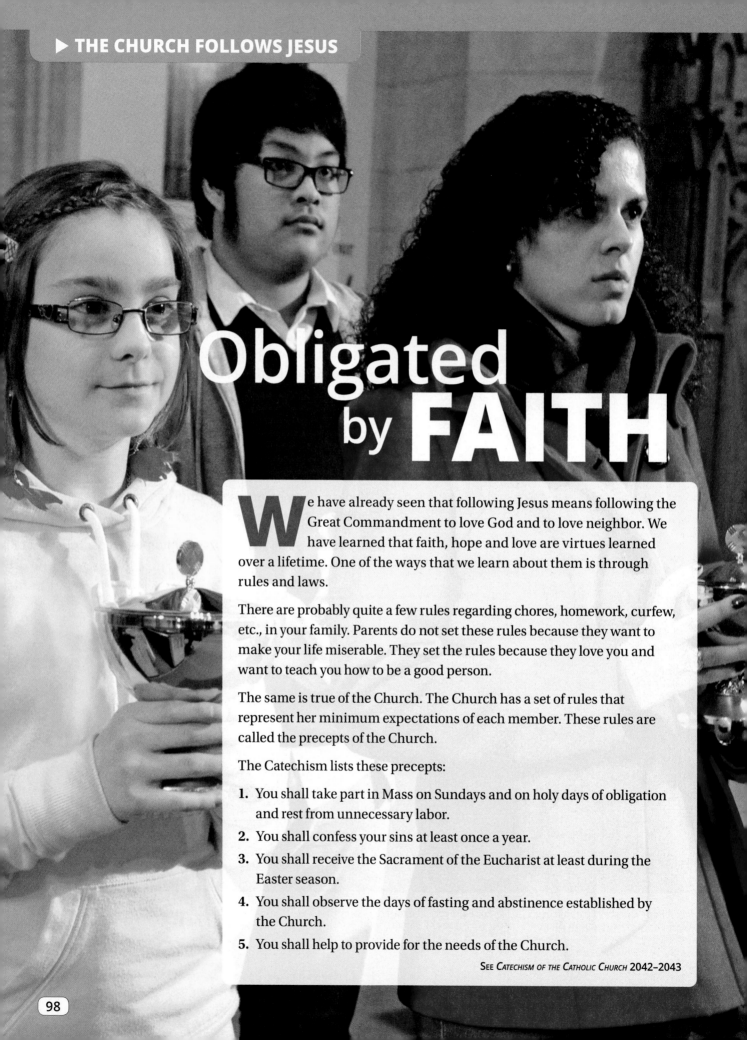

# Obligated by FAITH

**W**e have already seen that following Jesus means following the Great Commandment to love God and to love neighbor. We have learned that faith, hope and love are virtues learned over a lifetime. One of the ways that we learn about them is through rules and laws.

There are probably quite a few rules regarding chores, homework, curfew, etc., in your family. Parents do not set these rules because they want to make your life miserable. They set the rules because they love you and want to teach you how to be a good person.

The same is true of the Church. The Church has a set of rules that represent her minimum expectations of each member. These rules are called the precepts of the Church.

The Catechism lists these precepts:

1. You shall take part in Mass on Sundays and on holy days of obligation and rest from unnecessary labor.

2. You shall confess your sins at least once a year.

3. You shall receive the Sacrament of the Eucharist at least during the Easter season.

4. You shall observe the days of fasting and abstinence established by the Church.

5. You shall help to provide for the needs of the Church.

SEE *CATECHISM OF THE CATHOLIC CHURCH* 2042–2043

## Be with God

Every Catholic is obligated to follow these precepts, yet we need to realize that faith is not a checklist of rules. Following the rules of the Church means that we do so as an act of faith.

Taking part in Mass each week is more than attendance. We worship God because as our Creator, God is due our worship. We listen to the Word of God because our hearts long to hear him who is revealed. We participate in Mass because we need to be with God, in communion with him and the whole Church.

## Beyond the Minimum

Going to Confession once a year is the minimal obligation. The more strengthened we are by faith, the more compelled we are to take part in all aspects of the Church. We need spiritual discipline to feed our faith. Examining one's conscience on a regular basis is the starting point of developing the discipline of regularly celebrating the Sacrament of Penance and Reconciliation.

Receiving Holy Communion once a year during the Easter season is also the minimum. Frequent reception of the Eucharist is the best means of obtaining spiritual nourishment. The more we nurture our souls, the more spiritually healthy we become.

Fasting and abstaining applies mostly to the Lenten season, but we can challenge ourselves yearlong to live more simply. We can "fast" and "abstain" from distracting activities to keep us focused on what is most important in life.

▶ How often do you abstain from using electronic gadgets or surfing online?

Supporting the Church is not like paying for a movie. We are all members of the community and have the responsibility to help maintain her ministries and keep her mission thriving. We cannot have a functioning Church without the support of all her members. This support includes financial contributions, which are according to what one is able to afford. God calls us to sacrificially support the Church with our time, talents and treasures.

## FAITH JOURNAL

What precepts would you add to the ones listed on page 98?

▶ FAITH FOCUS

In what ways does God help us to live a good life?

▶ FAITH VOCABULARY

blasphemy

idols

perjury

reverence

## Written on Our Hearts

The Ten Commandments summarize the Law of God written on every human heart. This law is called the natural law. It is the foundation of all human laws, moral and civil. The Ten Commandments God revealed to Moses on Mount Sinai give us a clearer picture of that law.

## The Decalogue

The Ten Commandments are also called the Decalogue, which means "ten words." They are God's gift to the Israelites and to all people. The Decalogue is the foundation of our lives with God and with one another. In this sense, the Ten Commandments are the traditional and time-tested measure of a person's character. They are precepts that all people have a serious obligation to obey:

1. I am the Lord your God: you shall not have strange gods before me.

2. You shall not take the name of the Lord your God in vain.

3. Remember to keep holy the Lord's Day.

4. Honor your father and your mother.

5. You shall not kill.

6. You shall not commit adultery.

7. You shall not steal.

8. You shall not bear false witness against your neighbor.

9. You shall not covet your neighbor's wife.

10. You shall not covet your neighbor's goods.

▶ Describe the connection between the natural law and the Ten Commandments.

# The GIFT of GOD'S LAW

## Jesus and the Law

The revelation of the Law on Mount Sinai prepared the Israelites for the Revelation of Jesus Christ. Jesus, the Word of God, became flesh, and fulfilled the Revelation of the old law. Jesus taught his disciples:

> "Do not think that I have come to abolish the law or the prophets. I have come not to abolish but to fulfill. . . .
> [W]hoever obeys and teaches these commandments will be called greatest in the kingdom of heaven."
>
> MATTHEW 5:17, 19

Jesus called people to return to the way of their hearts—to love God and other people with their whole hearts (see Matthew 22:37–39). Paul stated it simply:

> [L]ove is the fulfillment of the law.
>
> ROMANS 13:10

Jesus did not only reveal the fulfillment of the Law. He also gave us the Holy Spirit to help us live the Law of God to its fullest. This New Testament prayer says it well:

> I kneel before the Father . . . that he may grant you . . . to be strengthened with power through his Spirit in the inner self, and that Christ may dwell in your hearts through faith; that you, rooted and grounded in love, may . . . know the love of Christ that surpasses knowledge, so that you may be filled with all the fullness of God.
>
> EPHESIANS 3:14, 16–19

## Faith CONNECTION

Working in a group, prepare a list of key rules that can help you live the Ten Commandments as Jesus taught. Then number your rules in order of their importance.

101

## The First Commandment

*I am the LORD your God: you shall not have strange gods before me.*

BASED ON EXODUS 20:2–3

The First Commandment commands us to set our priorities straight. Our first priority in life is God. We are to acknowledge the truth that God is God and that we are not. We are to believe in God, hope in God, and love God above all else in life.

The First Commandment is straightforward: Put God first and worship him alone. Throughout history and still today, the First Commandment is violated in many ways:

**Atheism.** Atheism is the rejection or denial of the existence of God.

**Idolatry.** Idolatry is worshiping **idols**, or false gods. An idol can be anything that takes the place of God in our lives. It can be someone or something that takes over a person's life. It can be money, power, fame, entertainment, technology or any other thing that becomes number one above God himself.

**Sacrilege.** Sacrilege consists of mistreating anyone or anything that is set aside, or consecrated, for worshiping God or helping people live as children of God.

**Superstition, divination, and magic.** Superstition, divination, and magic divert us from trusting in God's loving providence by claiming "special powers" on our own. Attributing some special ability or foresight to a false god is also a violation of the First Commandment.

**Simony.** Simony is the abuse of spiritual power or influence for personal gain.

All of these practices undermine true religion and belief in God.

▶ **What is the heart and center of the First Commandment?**

## DID YOU KNOW?

Statues, icons, and paintings in our churches help us worship God. Early in the history of the Church, a group of individuals called iconoclasts (image destroyers) started a campaign to destroy all sacred art representing God, Mary, angels, and Saints. The Second Council of Nicaea, however, taught the reason why Christians use sacred images: "Whoever venerates an image venerates the person portrayed in it" (see the *Catechism of the Catholic Church* 2132).

## The Second Commandment

*You shall not take the name of the* Lord *your God in vain.*

EXODUS 20:7

Respecting a person's name shows respect for that person. The Israelites had the highest form of respect, or **reverence**, for God and his very name. So great was the Israelites' reverence for God's name that his name was never to be spoken aloud. Thus the name of God, Yahweh, was abbreviated without the vowels as YHWH. The Israelites also substituted names such as "Lord" in place of YHWH.

Showing reverence for God's name is showing reverence for God himself. For Christians this is also true of the name and person of Jesus.

*God greatly exalted him*
*and bestowed on him the name*
  *that is above every name,*
*that at the name of Jesus*
*every knee should bend,*
*of those in heaven and on*
  *earth and under the earth,*
  *and every tongue confess that*
*Jesus Christ is Lord,*
*to the glory of God the Father.*

PHILIPPIANS 2:9–11

Speaking the name of God, Jesus, Mary, the Saints, or holy things in an offensive way is an act of irreverence. We call such acts of irreverence **blasphemy**. We also dishonor the name of God when we commit **perjury**. Perjury is the taking of a false oath by calling on God, who is Truth, to be a witness to a lie.

▶ Summarize the meaning of the First and Second Commandments in one sentence.

## The Third Commandment

*Remember to keep holy the Lord's Day.* BASED ON EXODUS 20:8

The Lord's Day is the day set aside to honor God. We keep this day holy by acknowledging the primacy of our relationship with God. We worship God and recreate our proper relationship with God, with our family, with others, and with all creation. We make sure that no other demands prevent us from making the observance of the Lord's Day the center of our week. Every Christian also has the obligation to avoid making demands on others that prevent them from observing the Lord's Day.

For Christians, Sunday is the Lord's Day. This day commemorates Christ's Resurrection, which is the beginning of the new creation of all things in Christ. The Sunday Mass is the heart of the Church's celebration of the Lord's Day. We join with Christ in unity with the Holy Spirit to pray the Church's great prayer of blessing and thanksgiving to God the Father and Creator. We remember and share in Christ's work of his making all things new through the saving events of his Paschal Mystery. We receive the grace, the nourishment, and the strength to show our reverence for God in all our words and actions.

So vital is our joining with the whole Church in celebrating the Eucharist that the Church obliges us to participate in its celebration on Sundays and other holy days of obligation. We can no more do without the spiritual nourishment of hearing the Word of God and partaking in the Eucharist on a regular basis, than we can do without the physical nourishment of food and drink.

## Faith CONNECTION

Illustrate a parish bulletin announcement proclaiming Sunday as the Lord's Day. Write the words of the headline in this space.

# STRANGE GODS AROUND

In society there are many slogans that claim happiness is found in the consumption of a certain product or in the possession of certain things. Such advertisements promise happiness in things. Things can turn into "strange gods" if we are not careful:

1. **Materialism** We all need some things in order to have a healthy and happy life. So material possessions in themselves are not bad, nor is having some things. Some things can definitely help bring joy in our lives or aid us in loving God, others and ourselves. But the constant pursuit of "more" can turn things into "strange gods," and too quickly they become idols.

2. **Vanity** As with material possessions, looking good is a worthy pursuit. However, when physical appearance becomes an obsession, the pursuit of beauty has turned to idol worship. A young teenager desiring to look beautiful is natural and normal. A young teenager consumed by the desire to look sexy is unhealthy and unworthy. God has gifted each of us with a natural beauty that we are to share with modesty and in humility.

3. **Profanity in Music** Imagine a world without music. Music is such a great gift that a life without it seems boring and awful. Young people develop their own specific tastes and favorites in music. That's good! But listen carefully to what you play. Some music is very degrading of people, promotes violence, or makes money or sex the meaning of life. In other words, some music actively promotes the profane and can easily become very "strange gods."

4. **Obsession in Sports** Sports are great! But some people get obsessed with sports and turn them into the center of their lives. It becomes all about winning at any cost. Use sports for fun competition, good exercise, opportunities for friendship, and ways of creating community.

▶ Which false gods or "strange gods" do you think teens struggle with most? Which do you struggle with most? What can you do to keep God at the center of your life?

# MY FAITH CHOICE

This week I will make God the first priority in my life. I will: _____

_____.

**PRAY** Lord, thank you for the gift of your laws that help us keep you first. Help me to make you my first priority today and always. Amen.

## Recall

*Define each of these faith terms:*

**1.** blasphemy _____

**2.** idols _____

**3.** perjury _____

**4.** reverence _____

*Choose two of the following questions to answer. Write a brief response for each.*

**5.** Describe the Ten Commandments as a summary of God's Law.

_____

_____

**6.** Why is the First Commandment the foundation of the other Commandments?

_____

_____

**7.** What is the connection between reverence and the Second Commandment?

_____

_____

## Reflect

*Using what you have learned in this chapter, briefly explain this statement:*
The Ten Commandments summarize the Law of God written on every human heart.

_____

_____

## Share

*Describe with a partner the importance of participating in Mass.*

_____

_____

### WITH MY FAMILY

Discuss with your family the following question:
Why is showing reverence for one another
important in the life of a family?

## To Help You
# REMEMBER

**1.** **The First Commandment demands that we place God first in our lives.**

**2.** **The Second Commandment calls on us to treat the name of God with respect and never invoke God's name inappropriately.**

**3.** **The Third Commandment calls on us to give time in prayer to God and to take part in Mass each Sunday.**

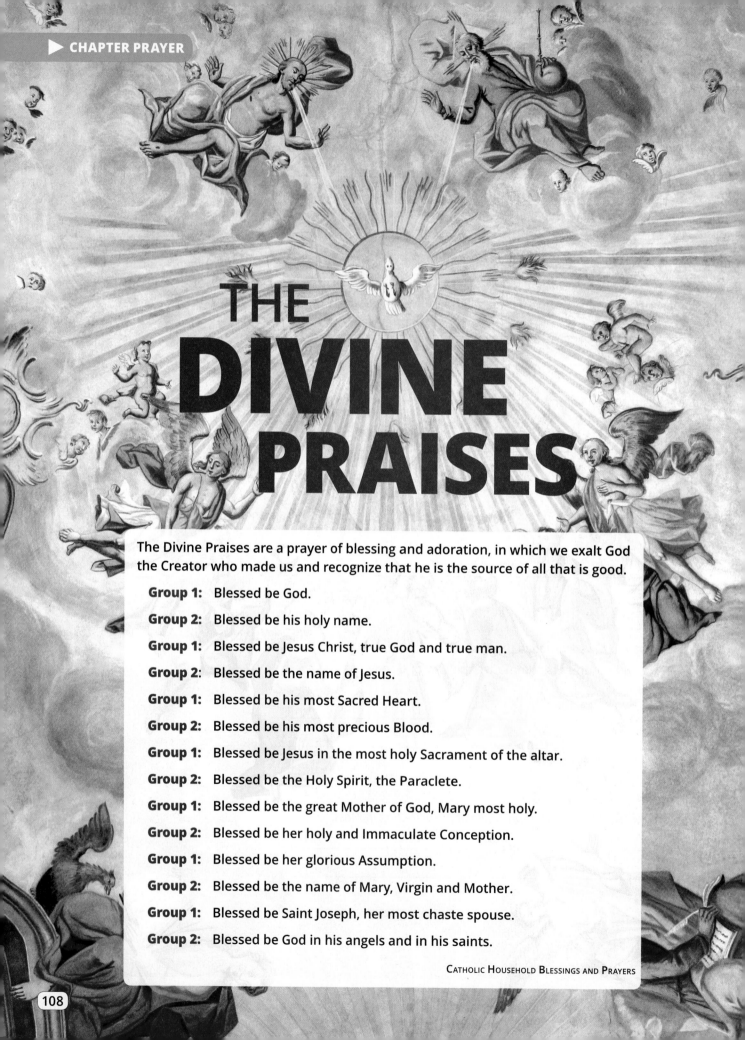

# THE DIVINE PRAISES

The Divine Praises are a prayer of blessing and adoration, in which we exalt God the Creator who made us and recognize that he is the source of all that is good.

**Group 1:** Blessed be God.

**Group 2:** Blessed be his holy name.

**Group 1:** Blessed be Jesus Christ, true God and true man.

**Group 2:** Blessed be the name of Jesus.

**Group 1:** Blessed be his most Sacred Heart.

**Group 2:** Blessed be his most precious Blood.

**Group 1:** Blessed be Jesus in the most holy Sacrament of the altar.

**Group 2:** Blessed be the Holy Spirit, the Paraclete.

**Group 1:** Blessed be the great Mother of God, Mary most holy.

**Group 2:** Blessed be her holy and Immaculate Conception.

**Group 1:** Blessed be her glorious Assumption.

**Group 2:** Blessed be the name of Mary, Virgin and Mother.

**Group 1:** Blessed be Saint Joseph, her most chaste spouse.

**Group 2:** Blessed be God in his angels and in his saints.

CATHOLIC HOUSEHOLD BLESSINGS AND PRAYERS

**LOOKING AHEAD**
In this chapter the Holy Spirit invites you to ▶

**EXPLORE** the work of the Community of Sant'Egidio.
**DISCOVER** the impact of the Commandments for us today.
**DECIDE** how you can become a disciple of peace.

CHAPTER **9**

# A **Community** for **Life**

▶ How do you stand up for life in your family?

Many people think that being pro-life means being opposed to abortion. This is true, but there is much more. We are called to have a consistent ethic of life. That is, we are to be pro-life in all that we do and say. Being pro-life is rooted in respect for the dignity of every human person—friend and foe, neighbor and stranger.

*I have set before you life and death, the blessing and the curse. Choose life, then, that you and your descendants may live.*

DEUTERONOMY 30:19

▶ Which teachings of the Church do you think are pro-life stances?

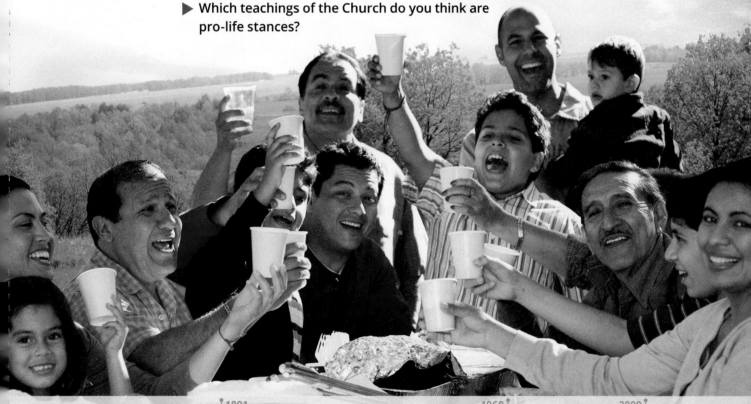

**TIMELINE**

| | | | |
|---|---|---|---|
| **1891** Pope Leo XIII teaches from *Rerum Novarum*. | **1968** Andrea Riccardi and friends form the Community of Sant'Egidio. | **2009** Pope Benedict XVI teaches from *Caritas in Veritate*. |

1850    1875    1900    1925    1950    1975    2000    2025

**1901** First Nobel Peace Prize is awarded.

**1982** UN establishes Sept. 21 as Day of Peace.

# A School for Peace

**W**e live in a world that is often overwhelmed by violence. Every day the news reports on some event of violence. Yet some are ignored. Each year more than a million abortions occur in the United States alone and an estimated 43 million worldwide. The atrocities continue. Both children and the elderly are far too often victims of physical abuse.

Yet in the midst of this violent world, there are many who are witnesses to peace. Countless Christians take a stand against such violence and hold dearly the sacredness of all human life. The Community of Sant'Egidio is such a group. This lay community of Catholic men and women throughout the world give witness to the power of faith as an instrument for peace.

## Service to the World

In 1968 some high school students in Rome who took seriously the challenge of the Church to become deeply engaged in the issues of the world began the community. They were convinced that service to the world was through both prayer and action.

▶ How is your service for others grounded in prayer?

The community began under the leadership of Andrea Riccardi and other students near the Piazza de Sant'Egidio in Trasteverde (a neighborhood of Rome, Italy). Their neighborhood was filled with the poor, and so their ministry began. These young peacemakers came together for prayer. They started an afternoon school to help others reflect on the life of Jesus. They established "schools of peace" among the poor.

Since that time, the community has increased globally and can be found in over 70 countries throughout the world, and includes nearly fifty thousand members. For the members of Sant'Egidio, the sacredness of all human life is more than a statement of belief, it is a way of living.

## Witnesses for Life

Sant'Egidio has been actively engaged in peacemaking throughout the world. Perhaps their most notable success was the resolution of a civil war in Mozambique, Africa in 1994 after sixteen years of civil war. The community continues to serve the needs in that country today.

Sant'Egidio realizes that the path to peace is through justice and compassion. The community seeks to serve the poor wherever they are. They take seriously Jesus' commandment to love everyone: the imprisoned, the poor, and those facing the death penalty.

▶ What other ways can we show love to everyone?

The community also honors the Fourth Commandment by respecting their elders and caring for the elderly and the infirmed. To respect others comes from the awareness and appreciation that every human being is created in the image and likeness of God.

Sant'Egidio is a remarkable group of Catholics who give witness to the Gospel of Life. They are a shining example of how faith-filled teens can live as disciples of Jesus. When young people wonder if they can make a difference in the world, the Community of Sant'Egidio reminds them: Yes, you can!

## FAITH JOURNAL

Imagine that you and your friends have begun a group to stand up as witnesses for life. Write your mission statement here:

_____

_____

_____

_____

_____

_____

_____

_____

_____

_____

_____

**▶ FAITH FOCUS**

What does the Church teach about how to respect human life?

**▶ FAITH VOCABULARY**

abortion

euthanasia

obedience

# HONOR and OBEY

## The Fourth Commandment

*Honor your father and your mother.* EXODUS 20:12

With this Commandment, God calls our attention to the whole family, including our elderly members. Our family is the most important community to which we belong. The family is the first place of prayer. The family is the heart and center of all other communities

The gift of children is a wonderful blessing to the family. By cooperating with God's plan for life and love, a husband and wife can participate in bringing the gift of new life into the world. So parents have a great duty to provide, as much as possible, for the physical and spiritual needs of their children. By word and example, Christian parents teach their children that the first calling of the Christian is to follow Christ. They are to respect, encourage, and support their children's vocations.

## Listen and Trust

Some children may think of the Fourth Commandment as an "overbearing" rule to obey their parents. But what does obey really mean? **Obedience** includes the respectful listening and trusting response to a person who has authority over us and who asks us to do something that is in accordance with God's Law or a just civil law.

When we obey the commands of our parents and trust in their guidance, we show the esteem in which we hold them. When we listen with respect, respond to their guidance with trust, and support them in their old age, we honor them. We build harmony in our families and strengthen the bonds that hold us together as a family.

God is quite clear. He lays down the law: After him, we are to honor and obey our parents, guardians, and those people who have the responsibility and authority for our growth and well-being.

▶ How is obeying your parents a way to honor them?

## The Civic Community

Civil authorities and citizens have responsibilities toward one another too. Civil authorities are those people who exercise legitimate authority in cities or towns and countries.

Civil authorities and citizens are to work together to build just and compassionate communities. The Church teaches that their tasks and responsibilities include:

- respecting all human life as sacred.

- respecting that the inherent rights of people flow from their dignity as persons created by God.

- protecting and fostering the inherent rights of every person without exception.

- guaranteeing conditions that promote and protect human life and freedom, and the peace and safety of all people.

- working to alleviate the unjust inequalities that exist between people.

- guarding against the dangers of a totalitarian society. A totalitarian society is a society in which one group of people exercises absolute control over everyone and uses falsehood and violence to govern.

Civil authorities sometime establish and enforce laws and policies that go against these principles. Our responsibility as citizens who are disciples of Christ is to work to change unjust and destructive policies. As the Word of God teaches,

*We must obey God rather than men.* ACTS 5:29

As citizens, we are to honor and respect civil authorities by (1) working with them in a spirit of truth and justice, (2) loving and serving our country, (3) paying taxes that support just activities, (4) and exercising our right to vote, and serving on juries.

The development of a human person occurs over a long period of time. At conception, new human life begins and continues to grow over different stages of development. After only 18 days, a baby's heart begins to beat. As early as 40 days, a baby's brainwaves can be detected. Various organs develop at different stages. Every person continues to grow and develop even after birth.

## The Fifth Commandment

*You shall not kill.*

Exodus 20:13

The Fifth Commandment demands that we respect and protect the sacredness of human life. God is the author of life. He creates every human person in his image and likeness. He shares his life and love with every person without exception. Without God's decision to share himself, there would be no life—no thing, no person would exist.

God's command to respect all human life as sacred is violated in many ways. Unfortunately, violence has become part of our world and has taken many forms. The Fifth Commandment calls us to stand against violence. God condemns and forbids the evils and grave sins that do violence to human life. Two examples include:

**Murder.** Murder is the direct and intentional killing of an innocent person. In all its forms, murder is always gravely sinful. Any cooperation in such an act as an accomplice is also seriously sinful.

**Abortion.** A child who is conceived, but not yet born, is still a person. Direct abortion, or the direct and intentional killing of an unborn child, is always gravely contrary to the moral law. This violent act violates the dignity of the human person and the holiness of the Creator.

A Catholic choosing to have an abortion or a Catholic performing or assisting in a direct abortion is excommunicated from the Church. This means that the person has chosen to separate himself or herself from the Church, and thereby must seek reconciliation with the Church according to the guidelines of his or her diocese before taking part in the Mass or receiving any sacrament. Also any Catholic who advocates for continued access to abortion violates the Fifth Commandment.

▶ **What can you do to stand against violence?**

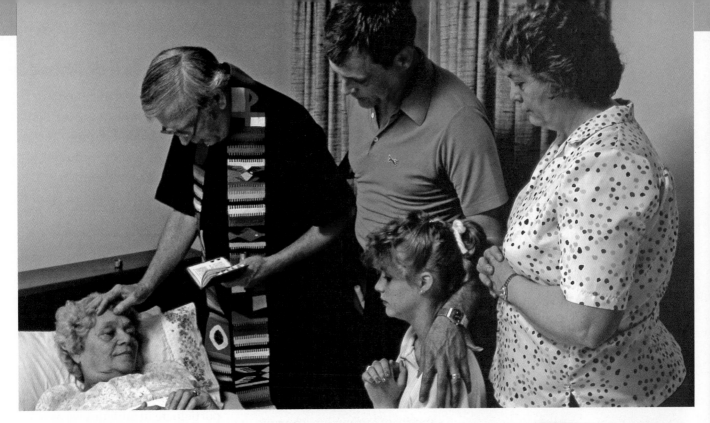

## Other Violations

Still there are many other examples of violence in the world. Some are more complex than others are. Nevertheless, we are to compassionately and reverently advocate for the respect of human life. Other examples of violent acts against human life include:

**Suicide.** Suicide is the intentional and direct killing of oneself. Suicide may reflect a sinful disregard for life, but often the person who commits suicide is overwhelmed by emotional pain or mental illness. The Church teaches that we are to show compassion for those hurting while still condemning wrongful acts. Hopefully through compassion, those hurting can find the help they need.

When a personal friend or member of a family commits suicide, the survivors experience overwhelming sadness and pain. Unanswered questions about the Salvation of our loved ones arise. We believe and trust that God in his loving mercy and forgiveness reaches out to those who take their own lives. When mental illness or emotional trauma are involved, people are not fully responsible for their actions.

**Euthanasia.** Euthanasia is the direct and intentional killing of a person who is suffering from a long-term or even terminal illness. Some people mistakenly believe that administering lethal drugs or helping suffering people administer lethal drugs to themselves is an act of mercy and compassion. Yet there is nothing compassionate about ending the life of an innocent though suffering person. The Church teaches that such an act is murder. It violates the dignity of the human person and the respect due to God, who is the author of life.

## Faith CONNECTION

Describe to a partner how direct abortion, suicide, or euthanasia are gravely wrong.

## Culture of Health

We are to show respect for the gift of our own lives by living healthy and holy lifestyles. Harmful or life-threatening behaviors, on the other hand, are acts of violence. They are against the sacredness of human life and the dignity of the human person.

We live responsibly with self-respect when we do not abuse prescription drugs, over-the-counter drugs, or alcohol. Drugs, including nicotine, are among the leading killers or accomplices in the deaths of both young people and adults. We defend the sanctity of human life when we stand against the use and selling of illegal drugs, such as cocaine and heroin.

We respect the gift of our lives when we eat healthy, exercise regularly, and responsibly care for our health. A proper diet is necessary as well.

## The Practice of Abuse

People can abuse their bodies through serious eating disorders characterized by a fear of weight gain leading to faulty eating habits, malnutrition, and excessive weight loss. Some athletes use steroids to build up muscles and strength. While this may lead to some initial strength benefits, it also results in lifetime losses for the human body. The abuse of steroids is a violation of the Fifth Commandment. So serious is this popular practice that athletes who use them are routinely declared ineligible to participate in athletic events.

▶ **What actions can you take to educate yourself on a healthier lifestyle?**

Unjust anger, hatred, prejudice, and the desire for revenge can lead to acts of violence against people. Civil wars, genocide, domestic violence, violent crimes, road rage, and shootings in schools and in workplaces are but a few examples of how such feelings and attitudes can lead to violent acts against others.

## Faith CONNECTION

Imagine that you are teaching a class to inform young people about the choices that show respect for their bodies and for one another. Decide on topics and key points for three sessions. Jot down the theme of each session here:

Session 1: _____

_____

Session 2: _____

_____

Session 3: _____

_____

# Violence versus PEACE

**Some people grow up thinking that violence is the only way to handle disagreements.** In your heart, you know that using violence to solve problems only begets more violence. As a Christian, you are called to be a disciple of peace, a peacemaker in conflict situations. Have you ever seen, heard, or been in any of these situations?

- You hear the loud, deafening sounds of video games blowing up skeletal people, shooting aliens, and firing missiles.

- Your brother or sister used your shirt without asking. You find it rolled up and dirty, thrown on the floor. You start yelling.

- Two men in a car accident get out of their cars and start cursing and pushing one another.

- You hear the news of another school shooting in which innocent people were killed and injured.

**Terminator or Perpetuator.** The word *terminator* at first seems to only have a violent meaning. The word literally means "one who puts an end to, or puts a stop to something." The word *perpetuator*, on the other hand, means "one who causes something to continue indefinitely." Here are a few steps to help you be the terminator of violence and the perpetuator of peace:

1. **Stop before acting hastily.** Name what you are feeling. Anger and embarrassment usually cause an explosive reaction. You may feel powerless or resentful. Cool down.

2. **Look at what happened.** Focus on the facts of the situation to see objectively. Can you accept your part of what happened?

3. **Listen to all sides to resolve the conflict.** Can you both look at the situation and think of a peaceful solution?

4. **Negotiate the best solution.** What do you have to do to make things better? Be willing to work through the difficulties for the sake of justice.

5. **Evaluate your handling of this situation.** If you were too assertive, you may have been selfish. If you were too compromising, you may have been exploited. Decide if a peace-filled action solved the problem.

> ▶ Discuss three reasons in favor of and three reasons opposed to a "zero-tolerance" policy.

# MY FAITH CHOICE

This week I will be a peaceful problem solver. I will: _____

_____.

**PRAY** Holy Spirit, Lord of Life, give me the courage to take a stand for the sanctity of human life. Amen.

## Recall

*Define each of these faith terms:*

**1.** abortion _____

**2.** euthanasia _____

**3.** obedience _____

*Write a brief response for each of these questions.*

**4.** Describe how obedience is different when it comes from a human being than when from a pet.

_____

_____

**5.** Explain how living the Fourth Commandment builds strong families and strong civil communities.

_____

_____

## Reflect

*Using what you have learned in this chapter, briefly explain this statement:*

*Blessed are the peacemakers,*
*for they will be called children of God.*

MATTHEW 5:9

_____

_____

_____

## Share

*Describe to a partner how the Fifth Commandment helps us respect the sacredness of our own lives and the lives of others.*

## WITH MY FAMILY

Discuss with your family the following question, "What are some of the ways we show respect for one another?"

### To Help You
# REMEMBER

**1.** The Fourth Commandment means that we must obey those in just authority with respect.

**2.** The Fifth Commandment demands that we treat all human life as sacred.

**3.** We are called to work together to defend the sanctity of human life by being peace-filled disciples of Jesus.

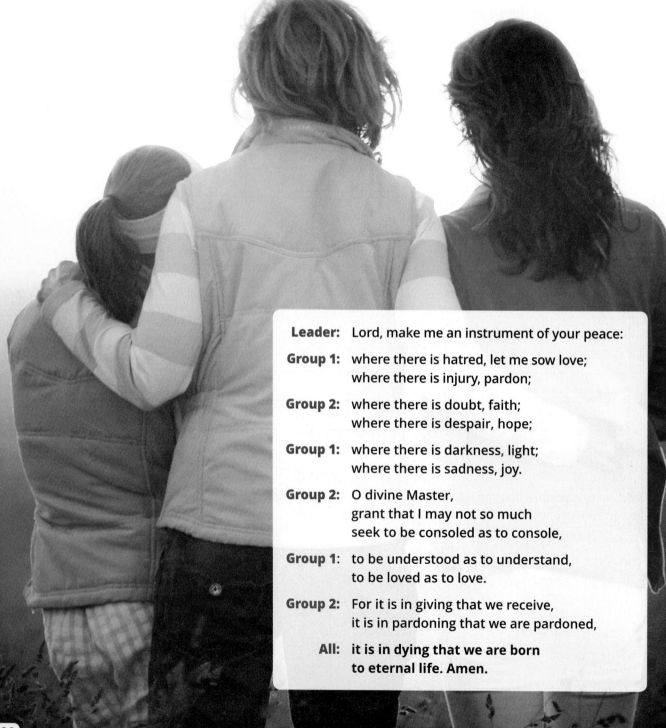

# Prayer for PEACE

**Leader:** Lord, make me an instrument of your peace:

**Group 1:** where there is hatred, let me sow love;
where there is injury, pardon;

**Group 2:** where there is doubt, faith;
where there is despair, hope;

**Group 1:** where there is darkness, light;
where there is sadness, joy.

**Group 2:** O divine Master,
grant that I may not so much
seek to be consoled as to console,

**Group 1:** to be understood as to understand,
to be loved as to love.

**Group 2:** For it is in giving that we receive,
it is in pardoning that we are pardoned,

**All:** it is in dying that we are born
to eternal life. Amen.

LOOKING AHEAD

In this chapter the Holy
Spirit invites you to ▶

EXPLORE the way faith can transform marriage.

DISCOVER how to live with integrity and generosity.

DECIDE on which values to support in the media.

CHAPTER **10**

# Integrity
## of
# Heart

▶ **How do you view yourself and those around you?**

Every day we are bombarded with images and sounds that communicate a message with a purpose. Some of these media messages respect us as persons. Often though, these messages distort the image in which God created us. God desires for us all that is true, good, and beautiful:

*Love justice, you who judge the earth;*
*think of the LORD in goodness,*
*and seek him in integrity of heart.*

WISDOM 1:1

▶ **What does "integrity of heart" mean to you?**

**TIMELINE**

| | |
|---|---|
| 480–547 | Life of Saint Benedict of Nursia |
| 1979–1984 | Pope John Paul II gives a series of lectures on theology of the body. |
| 2010 | Pope Benedict XVI gives his World Day of Peace message. |

400     800     1950     2000     2050

1971
First coin-operated video game, Galaxy Game, is made.

1982
UN establishes October 16 as World Food Day.

# Witnessing Love

One of the beautiful things about the Church is her amazing diversity. Many cultures are expressed in the Catholic Church. So many different kinds of people make up the Church—including all types of married couples. The following examples represent some of the many ways in which married couples share their love with each other and faithfully serve the Church in the world.

## The Rule of Hospitality

David and Karen live outside Washington, D.C. in a nice suburban community. David is a successful entrepreneur, and his wife Karen is in health-care management. Yet they are most respected for their active involvement in the community. David and Karen are known as the hospitality couple. Through their service to others, they demonstrate their fidelity to God.

On the weekends, David drives a van filled with sandwiches and soup to certain "rest stops" where the homeless await him. David has a lot of personality and can make anyone laugh. He brings joy as well as food to those in need. Karen is the ultimate mom, capable of juggling a million tasks and being present at all the events in her children's very busy lives. She is also the ultimate host, who welcomes

*Hospes venit, Christus venit*

guests and opens the door at the local shelter that she and her husband began ten years ago. Above the front door is a sign bearing the shelter's motto: *Hospes venit; Christus venit*. This means "When a guest comes, Christ comes."

This rule of hospitality first attributed to Saint Benedict has helped David and Karen to serve their family and community. They show love to others as if each person they encounter is Christ.

## Dispensing Grace

Maria and Eduardo are a young married couple, not yet thirty, of Mayan ancestry. They both have well-paying jobs, yet they choose to live simply. For example, Maria's wedding ring is a simple Mayan-style copper wire ring that cost about two dollars. Her ring is a reminder of their faithfulness to their families as well as a sign of fidelity between her and Eduardo. They are bright, athletic, caring, and fun. Anyone who meets them knows quickly that the center of their life is their Catholic faith. They know in their hearts that their Catholic faith brings them great joy.

Their simple personal lifestyle affords them opportunities to do missionary work during their vacations. They experience great joy in sharing with others what God has provided for them. Each year they travel to Central America to visit clinics that their parish supports. Eduardo, a medical doctor, works in the clinics, while Maria, a registered nurse, helps dispense important vaccination shots. They both imagine that through their little contributions they are providing God's healing grace to those who would otherwise never receive such necessary medical attention.

## A Family of Faith

Joe and Lucy are in their early seventies. Lucy volunteers to bring meals to elderly who are homebound, and Joe still "signs" at Mass for the deaf community. They are proud grandparents to fifteen grandchildren. Some of them are adopted, and some have special needs, like Down syndrome. Joe and Lucy are proud of their children and grandchildren, who remind them daily of the love they share with one another. Through fifty years, their marriage has given witness to their love for each other and their faith in God.

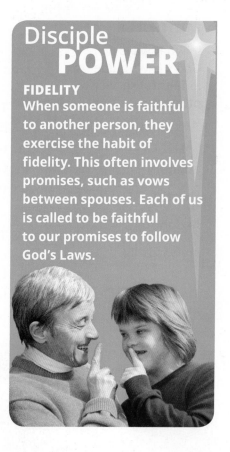

## Disciple POWER

**FIDELITY**
When someone is faithful to another person, they exercise the habit of fidelity. This often involves promises, such as vows between spouses. Each of us is called to be faithful to our promises to follow God's Laws.

## FAITH JOURNAL

Reflect on your own family life. Write about ways you and your family witness to others the love you have received from God.

▶ FAITH FOCUS

In what ways do God's Laws guide us in faithful service to others?

▶ FAITH VOCABULARY

adultery

chastity

hedonism

stewardship

## The Sixth and Ninth Commandments

*You shall not commit adultery.*
*You shall not covet your neighbor's wife.*     Exodus 20:14, 17

The Sixth and Ninth Commandments are related to God's plan for life and love. These Laws of God guide us to respect each other in our relationships and help us stay true to God's plan for human sexuality. God has created each of us either male or female. Through healthy, loving relationships we mature in our appreciation for who God created us to be.

Sexuality is God's gift of being a man or a woman, a boy or a girl. Through our sexuality, we express and share our innermost being with others. Because our sexuality expresses who we are most intimately, God encourages us to virtuously live out our sexuality. He calls us to honor and guard our "true selves" so we can keep integrity of heart. Some of these virtues include:

- **Prudence.** Our sexuality is good and a gift from God. Like with any gift, this unique gift can be cherished wisely or used foolishly.

- **Self-control.** Our sexuality grows and develops over time. The wise and loving use of our sexuality means that we must know ourselves and discipline ourselves.

- **Chastity.** We need to respect the sexuality of others and ourselves. This can be very challenging today. **Hedonism** abounds in advertisements and is all too often culturally acceptable. This leads many people to make unwise and sometimes damaging choices.

## Honor One Another

Women and men possess differences that balance and complete each other. Learn to recognize the ways in which men and women, boys and girls, complement each other. This is part of God's plan for our sexuality. Men and women are equal in dignity and complementary in gender. When we honor these differences as images of truth, beauty and goodness, we respect each other as God created us. And in God's plan for marriage, the intimate exchange of sexual love is reserved for marriage when a man and a woman have promised to faithfully love each other.

# FAITHFUL SERVICE

## Catholics
# BELIEVE

Through Baptism, we receive the gift of the Holy Spirit who enables us and strengthens us to hold onto or restore purity of heart. Purity needs modesty, and modesty requires temperance. Modesty protects that beautiful person God sees in each of us.

## Living a Chaste Life

Everyone is obliged to live a chaste life. The virtue of chastity guides us in expressing our sexuality properly according to our state in life. Chastity involves the persistent habit of self-mastery and the controlling of our passions. Christ is the model for living a chaste life. All who are baptized into Christ receive the grace of the Holy Spirit to live chaste lives. Some good practical advice on how to maintain a chaste life includes:

- **Choose temperance.** This Cardinal Virtue helps us respond appropriately in making decisions, including ones based on the desire to love and be loved. Being temperate means practicing self-control and self-discipline. You can resist the temptations of indulgence and immediate gratification, despite how others treat you.

- **Live modesty.** This good habit helps preserve your innermost self for only those who truly love you for who you are. A modest person is inspired to be discreet in behavior and reserved in attire so as to honor the mystery of the inner self. You can resist the cultural pressures of voyeurism and allurements of sexual exploitations. Much of the mass media, especially online resources, routinely glamorize unrestrained sexual exhibitionism. This behavior is contrary to God's plan for us and violates Gospel values.

- **Beware of fantasizing about another person.** Fantasizing may lead to coveting. In the Ninth Commandment *covet* means to desire another person, married or unmarried, for one's own personal sexual pleasure. Acting immodestly may also lead to coveting.

- **Avoid sexual activity outside of marriage.** Non-marital sex, **adultery**, fornication, cohabitation, homosexual practices, and masturbation are not part of God's plan for human sexuality. These activities contradict Christian purity and disrespect integrity of heart.

## Faith
# CONNECTION

Imagine that you are asked to prepare a photo article for a teen magazine showing young people living the Sixth Commandment. Describe to a partner two pictures your article would feature.

## The Seventh Commandment

*You shall not steal.*                                    Exodus 20:15

This Commandment teaches that all creation belongs first of all to God the Creator. He is the source of all life, everything visible and invisible. God created the world for the benefit of all. God has made us stewards of creation. Through our work we participate in the very work of God the Creator. Because we are joined to Christ in Baptism, our work is to be united to Christ, the Redeemer, and is to give glory and praise to the Father.

We are privileged to care for God's creation and are not to usurp its ownership from God. This is what we refer to as **stewardship**. Creation is ours to use, not to abuse. Creation is ours to share generously, not to hoard selfishly.

▶ How can you be a good steward of God's creation?

The Seventh Commandment tells us to fulfill responsibly the command God gave to each of us individually and to all of us as his family:

*Have dominion over the fish of the sea, the birds of the air, and all the living things that move on the earth.*                    Genesis 1:28

## Stewards in the World

Stewardship is the managing of and caring for the property of another person. The stewardship of God's creation involves these concerns:

- **Concern for the future.** God gave us the whole world for everyone's use. We are to use it wisely and unselfishly. We are to use it and enjoy it, keeping others in mind, especially those in most need or vulnerable. We are not to consume its resources for our own generation's profit and comfort to the detriment of future generations. This would in effect steal from them and disrespect the gift of creation, which God has given to all of humanity.

- **Concern for the poor.** We serve Christ when we share our blessings with people in need (see Matthew 25:31–46). Good stewards act justly. They do not work to amass more and more at the expense of others. Sharing acts are works of justice that are pleasing to God. The Church has a preferential love for those who are oppressed by poverty or vulnerable to the selfishness of society. The Church labors around the world to relieve, defend, and liberate the oppressed and vulnerable.

■ **Concern for the common good.** We are a global family. God's children live all over the world. By reaching out to people in need, wherever they live, we are fulfilling our responsibility to act justly as stewards of God's creation.

■ **Concern for public life.** We have a responsibility to take an active part in public life. We are to share our material blessings and our talents with others. Failure to vote, failure to contribute time for public service, and failure to lend our voices to matters of justice and the welfare of fellow citizens essentially rob society of what is due to all, a just and good life.

▶ Why is it everyone's responsibility to help those suffering from starvation, poverty, and disease?

## Stealing Dignity

The Seventh Commandment demands that we treat people justly. Stealing is an act of injustice. It is the taking or abusing of the possessions that rightfully and legitimately belong to another person. The word *possessions* in this description includes much more than material things people have. Here are some examples of stealing:

- Wage earners who are not given a just wage for their work.
- The deliberate withholding of a lost item by a person who is not the rightful owner.
- The willful damage of what belongs to another.
- Cheating on a test, or taking another's knowledge or ideas and claiming it as one's own.
- Discrimination in employment because of age, gender, culture, ethnicity, religion, disability, or economic status.
- Increasing the profits and power of a few individuals at the expense of others.
- Slavery or human trafficking, which robs human beings of their freedom and reduces God's children to some commodity, a status like some merchandise.

All forms of stealing are acts of disrespect toward the dignity of the human person. They are acts of injustice that demand reparation. If we steal something, we must return it and take responsibility for having done wrong. If we damage someone else's property, we must offer to have it repaired. If we lose someone else's property, we must offer to replace it. If we have helped someone steal or benefited from a theft, we must make amends.

### Faith CONNECTION

Choose one of these three issues: stealing, vandalism, or cheating. Work with a partner to design a positive strategy for dealing with the issue in your parish or school.

# TEMPTING
## Messages

Many false messages in the media tempt us away from faithfully living God's Commandments.

*Do you believe that you are strongly influenced by the media? Does society encourage you to live a good Christian life? Do messages in the media sometimes make it more difficult for you to live the Gospel?*

Here are a few messages that you probably see or hear quite often. If you strongly agree, circle SA, strongly agree; A, agree; D, disagree; or SD, strongly disagree. Then share with the class the reasons for your choices.

1. Physical beauty is very important.

   SA    A    D    SD

2. Wealth is the sign of happiness.

   SA    A    D    SD

3. Violence on television and in the movies can have a negative effect on people.

   SA    A    D    SD

4. Society says the same thing that Jesus said about love and commitment.

   SA    A    D    SD

5. Sexual activity outside of marriage is okay as long as both partners agree.

   SA    A    D    SD

# BE A TRUTH SEEKER

**Certain messages in the media will try to convince you** that they are telling you the truth and that they always have your best interests at heart. Do you believe this? Start to evaluate the messages you hear. Determine the real intent. Are the values being communicated important to you? Are these messages aligned with God's Commandments? Seek the truth in the media and be influenced by Gospel values.

_____

_____

In a small group discuss your favorite movie, video, show or song. Describe how its values respect or reject the Sixth, Seventh, or Ninth Commandments.

_____

_____

_____

_____

_____

_____

_____

_____

## MY FAITH CHOICE

This week I will focus on only those media messages that encourage me to follow God's Laws. I will: _____

_____ .

**PRAY** God our Creator, I praise you for the beautiful gift of your creation. Help me to faithfully serve, honor and love this gift, especially those people whom I encounter today. Amen.

## Recall

*Define each of these faith terms:*

**1.** chastity _____

**2.** hedonism _____

**3.** stewardship _____

**4.** adultery _____

*Choose two of the following questions to answer. Write a brief response for each of your choices.*

**5.** Discuss ways you can respect and honor your gift of sexuality.

_____

_____

**6.** Explain how stealing is an act of disrespect.

_____

_____

**7.** Explain what it means to care for God's creation.

_____

_____

## Reflect

*Using what you have learned in this chapter, briefly explain this statement:*

*"[The body] speaks by means of its masculinity and femininity. It speaks in the mysterious language of the personal gift . . . [the body speaks\ in the language of fidelity.".*

POPE JOHN PAUL II, THE LANGUAGE OF THE BODY IN THE STRUCTURE OF MARRIAGE

_____

_____

## Share

*Explain to a partner the principles that help you live a chaste life.*

## WITH MY FAMILY

Discuss with your family the following question, "How do we as a family show others integrity of heart?

### To Help You
# REMEMBER

**1.** Our sexuality is a gift from God to be lived through chaste living.

**2.** Marriage is the only proper relationship for sexual activity.

**3.** All forms of stealing are sins against human dignity.

WE RECYCLE

# IF I HAVE
# LOVE

**Leader:** Let us love not in word or speech but in deed and truth.      1 John 3:18

**Group 1:** If I speak in human and angelic tongues, but do not have love, I am a resounding gong or a clashing cymbal.

**Group 2:** And if I have the gift of prophecy and comprehend all mysteries and all knowledge; if I have all faith so as to move mountains, but do not have love, I am nothing.

**Group 1:** If I give away everything I own, and if I hand my body over so that I may boast but do not have love, I gain nothing.

**Group 2:** Love is patient, love is kind. It is not jealous, [love] is not pompous, it is not inflated, it is not rude, it does not seek its own interests.

**Group 1:** [I]t is not quick-tempered, it does not brood over injury, it does not rejoice over wrongdoing but rejoices with the truth.

**Group 2:** It bears all things, believes all things, hopes all things, endures all things.

**Group 1:** So faith, hope, love remain, these three; but the greatest of these is love.

1 Corinthians 13:1–7, 13

**All:** Amen.

LOOKING AHEAD
In this chapter the Holy Spirit invites you to ▶

EXPLORE the courage of being a disciple of Jesus.
DISCOVER how God's Laws demand honesty.
DECIDE how to positively influence friends.

CHAPTER 11

# People of Truth

▶ **What challenges have you faced in being honest and generous?**

An eleven-year-old contestant made it to the fourth round of a national spelling contest. The contestant had to spell *avowal*. After doing so, the judges were not able to agree on whether an "a" or an "e" was used for the second-to-last letter. Finally, the chief judge asked, "How did you spell the word?" The contestant admitted, "I misspelled the word" and graciously left the stage.

> Make known to me your ways, LORD;
>    teach me your paths.
> Guide me in your truth and teach me,
>    for you are God my savior.     PSALM 25:4–5

▶ **How do you find the courage to do what is right and true?**

| TIMELINE | | | | | |
|---|---|---|---|---|---|
| | **1181–1226** Life of Saint Francis of Assisi | | **1469–1535** Life of Saint John Fisher | **1478–1535** Life of Saint Thomas More | |
| 1150 | 1200 | 1300 | 1400 | 1500 | 1600 |
| | | | **1472** Dante Alighieri's *The Divine Comedy* is published. | **1509–1547** Reign of King Henry VIII of England | |

# A Stand for Truth

**T**ruth and integrity are among the most important qualities we can have. Telling the truth is sometimes very difficult. Lying may often seem easier. So having the courage to do what is right, telling the truth, is important.

Sir Thomas More was a man known for his honesty and integrity. He was a lawyer in England during the reign of King Henry VIII. More was an intellectual widely admired throughout Europe and a judge known for his integrity. Like many Catholics of that time, More knew that the Church was in need of reform, yet he understood some of the ideas and actions of Martin Luther were wrong. He helped King Henry VIII write an essay entitled *In Defense of the Seven Sacraments*.

Ironically, the king found himself in a disagreement with Pope Clement VII. Henry needed an heir to the throne and wanted the Pope to grant him an annulment from his wife, Catherine of Aragon, in order to marry Anne Boleyn. Growing impatient, Henry declared himself the head of the Church in England and gave himself the annulment.

By this time, Thomas More had become the Lord Chancellor of England, the second most powerful man in the realm. In response to the king's actions, More resigned from his position as Chancellor and refused to sign the oath of supremacy, which declared the king head of the Church in England. More was imprisoned in the Tower of London, and was eventually beheaded when Sir Richard Rich falsely testified against him.

▶ **Could you courageously stand up for honesty and integrity like More?**

been beheaded for questioning the marriage of Herod to his brother's divorced wife, Herodias. Like his patron, Fisher was beheaded for similar reasons.

A disciple of Jesus is someone who can be trusted to speak the truth. Both Thomas More and John Fisher were canonized as Saints in 1935. Their feast day is celebrated together on June 22.

## Respected for Honesty

The famous story of Saint Thomas More became internationally popular in the play and film, *A Man for All Seasons*. The movie, released in 1966, won six Oscars including best picture. The film focuses on More's honesty, integrity and faithfulness to his conscience.

More was not the only prominent Catholic to refuse to take the king's oath of supremacy. Bishop John Fisher also had a friendly relationship with King Henry VIII. He was one of only a few bishops who stood up against the king's marriage to Anne Boleyn. Like More, Bishop Fisher was also widely respected throughout Europe. His integrity was unquestioned throughout his life, and his letters indicate that he was thoroughly fearless in his defense of the authority of the Pope. His patron Saint, John the Baptist, had

*A Man for All Seasons* (1966): Paul Scofield as Sir Thomas More (center) and John Hurt as Sir Richard Rich (far right)

## FAITH JOURNAL

What lessons do you take away from reading about the courageous stances of More and Fisher? How might their lives be an inspiration for you?

▶ **FAITH FOCUS**

How does God's Law guide us to be people of truth and integrity?

---

▶ **FAITH VOCABULARY**

covet

envy

generosity

integrity

lying

## The Eighth Commandment

*You shall not bear false witness against your neighbor.*

EXODUS 20:16

The Jewish legal system was based on this Commandment. One took an oath to tell the truth because lying was expected otherwise. The oath was the promise to God and to the community to tell the truth. Jesus taught what is at the heart of this Commandment when he said,

*"But I say to you, do not swear at all . . . Let your 'Yes' mean 'Yes,' and your 'No' mean 'No.' Anything more is from the evil one."*

MATTHEW 5:34, 37

## Living the Truth

Jesus taught his disciples to be truthful in all things. His followers never need to take an oath because they are to speak the truth always. Jesus taught at the heart of this Commandment is the integrity of truth. Truth will always set us free to live as God created us to live. Jesus said,

*"If you remain in my word, you will truly be my disciples, and you will know the truth, and the truth will set you free."*  JOHN 8:31–32

▶ **How has telling the truth set you free?**

Telling the truth is easy when the truth is one of which we are proud. Telling the truth is difficult, however, when we have done something wrong. That is why there is a connection between honesty and integrity. Honesty is speaking the truth. **Integrity** is living the truth. Integrity means being true with our words and in our actions.

## Bearing False Witness

Telling the truth requires practice. So does telling lies, or bearing false witness. **Lying** is the act of intentionally deceiving someone who has the right to the truth by deliberately saying what is false.

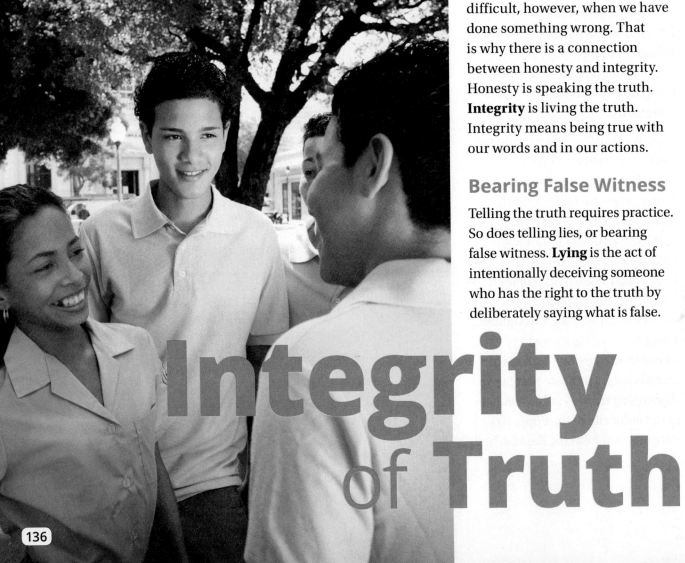

# Integrity of Truth

## DID YOU KNOW?

People bear false witness against the Jewish people when they state that all Jewish people, including Jewish people today, are guilty of the crimes committed during Christ's Passion. This is a form of anti-Semitism, which the Church condemns.

Given enough time and practice, any of us can become experienced or habitual liars. There are several ways that we can bend, twist, distort, or even destroy the truth:

- **Perjury.** Perjury is lying under oath.

- **Gossip.** Harming a person's reputation and honor typically happens through gossip.

- **Boasting.** Some people try to earn recognition by unnecessarily inflating their accomplishments and abilities.

▶ How have you been affected by another's lie?

Rash judgment occurs when we rush to judge another person's moral standing without sufficient reasons or evidence. Detraction is the unjust revealing to a third party of someone else's faults or failings. Calumny is the making of untrue remarks that leads to doubting or questioning another person's reputation or honor. These acts violate the Eighth Commandment.

## Keeping Confidence

There are situations that demand that we remain silent and not share what we know to be true.

We are not obligated to reveal the truth to someone who does not have a right to know it. In fact, in some situations we might even have an obligation not to disclose the truth we know. For example, the sacramental seal of confession can never be broken. The secrecy and confidentiality of conversations between lawyers and their clients are protected by civil law. The good and safety of other people, the common good, and respect for privacy may be sufficient reasons for remaining silent and not sharing what we know to be true.

## Justice Demands Truth

Telling the truth is vital to our relationships with people. Telling lies tears down trust and separates people from one another. Telling the truth is so important that justice demands we repair the damage or harm caused by our acts against the truth. When we lie, we must make amends to those whom we have caused harm, including God. Justice demands that we reconcile our relationships. With God, we can find reconciliation in the Sacrament of Penance and Reconciliation.

## Faith CONNECTION

Role-play with a partner a scenario in which it is difficult and embarrassing to tell the truth.

## The Tenth Commandment

*You shall not covet your neighbor's goods.* BASED ON EXODUS 20:17

The Tenth Commandment guides us in keeping our hearts in the right place. When we **covet** another person's goods, we wrongfully treasure that person's possessions, abilities, talents, friends, achievements, and so on. To covet can be a mix of different sins. We may crave the blessings of others out of **envy**; or we may lust after the person because of selfish desires; or we may seek in greed their possessions.

## Seven Deadly Sins

The Church teaches us that there are seven Capital Sins, or sins that are at the root of other sins. They are sometimes referred to as "deadly" sins because of the serious damage they do to the truth and our relationships. These sins are often interrelated, one leading to another. The Church has named seven Capital Sins: pride, covetousness (greed), lust, anger (wrath), gluttony, envy, and sloth (laziness).

**Greed.** The unchecked desire to have more and more things is greed, also called avarice or covetousness. Greed is an excessive passion for wealth and the status or power often connected with wealth. It distorts the truth, turning possessions into idols. An avaricious person never seems to have enough. If you analyze the news, you will see how the lives of avaricious people are marked by fraud, theft, and other criminal behaviors.

For some people, greed becomes a compulsion to have more, the latest, or the trendiest things they can buy. Moreover, often greed builds off envy and vice versa.

**Envy.** We can be blind to the truth that all blessings come from God. Envious people are saddened that other people have something they do not have. Envy can lead to hatred of neighbors, telling lies about them, harming their reputations, and even rejoicing at their misfortune. Humility, goodwill, and trust in Divine Providence help us to see the goodness of our own lives and overcome the temptation of envy (read Matthew 4:7–10, 6:25–34).

▶ What examples of greed or envy have you witnessed?

Faith
**CONNECTION**

Describe characters from books or movies who act out one of the seven deadly sins as related to violating the Tenth Commandment. Give examples and describe the consequences of their actions.

## Heart Condition

In his teaching, Jesus was always concerned about the condition of our hearts. He often echoed the words from Psalm 95 and from Isaiah imploring us not to harden our hearts (read Mark 10:5, John 12:40). In Matthew 6:19–21 Jesus tells us to keep our priorities straight. By working harder at filling our hearts with earthly things rather than that of God, we are setting ourselves up for a spiritual heart attack.

*"For where your treasure is, there also will your heart be."* MATTHEW 6:21

## Destination: Heaven

If we want our lives with God to thrive, we cannot become consumed by worldly possessions. If we are consumed with this world, we will be unable to focus on that which leads us to God. We need to develop the habit of **generosity**. We need to use possessions for what God has in store for us. The blessings we receive, including wealth, are for the benefit of others and ourselves. Success is not defined by the accumulation of things, but by the generosity of hearts. As disciples of Jesus, we are to give to others for the betterment of all. With humble and generous hearts, we set our destination to Heaven.

## Faith CONNECTION

Look up these three Scripture passages. Choose one and describe how it can guide a follower of Jesus to live the Gospel.

| SCRIPTURE PASSAGE | FOLLOWING CHRIST |
| --- | --- |
| Chronicles 29:10–14 | |
| Mark 12:41–44 | |
| Corinthians 9:6–8 | |

# Peer PRESSURE

We usually think of peer pressure as negative, but it can also be positive. As a negative, peer pressure moves one to wrongly go along with the crowd, even if it means going against one's better judgment. In the positive sense, peer pressure can influence you to do what is right and make good choices at times when you need courage.

## NEGATIVE PRESSURE

**Here are a few examples of negative peer pressure:**

■ **Collusion** is an agreement that a few people make for a wrong or evil purpose. Usually it means they make up a lie or a rumor and try to convince others to go along with it. For example. talking about people behind their backs or starting false rumors about others can ruin the reputation of those people or hurt them deeply.

■ **Bullies** try to boss, threaten, and control others. Bullies pick on or make fun of other students who may then become outcasts of the class and the brunt of cruel jokes.

■ **Mobs** occur when a crowd decides to do something you know is wrong or something you would never choose to do on your own. It is difficult to resist one person's influence. It is even harder to go against an entire group.

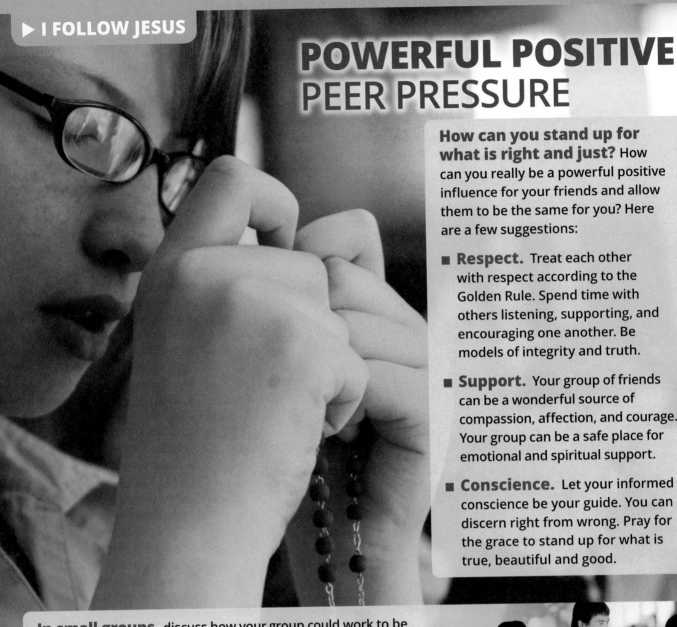

# POWERFUL POSITIVE
## PEER PRESSURE

**How can you stand up for what is right and just?** How can you really be a powerful positive influence for your friends and allow them to be the same for you? Here are a few suggestions:

■ **Respect.** Treat each other with respect according to the Golden Rule. Spend time with others listening, supporting, and encouraging one another. Be models of integrity and truth.

■ **Support.** Your group of friends can be a wonderful source of compassion, affection, and courage. Your group can be a safe place for emotional and spiritual support.

■ **Conscience.** Let your informed conscience be your guide. You can discern right from wrong. Pray for the grace to stand up for what is true, beautiful and good.

**In small groups,** discuss how your group could work to be a positive influence among your peers. How would observing the Ten Commandments help you achieve this goal? What challenges might you face?

_____

_____

# MY FAITH CHOICE

This week I will ask the Holy Spirit to give me the courage to be a person of integrity and truth. I will: _____

_____ .

**PRAY** Come Holy Spirit, enliven in me the courage to avoid the occasion of sin so that I may be a person of truth. Amen.

## Recall

*Define each of these faith terms:*

**1.** integrity _____

**2.** courage _____

**3.** covet _____

**4.** envy _____

**5.** greed _____

*Choose one of the following questions to answer. Write a brief response for your choice.*

**6.** Explain what "bearing false witness" means.

_____

_____

**7.** Explain the sinfulness of covetousness.

_____

_____

## Reflect

*Using what you have learned in this chapter, briefly explain this statement:*

*"For where your treasure is, there also will your heart be."*

MATTHEW 6:21

_____

_____

## Share

*Describe to a partner how the Tenth Commandment guides us in living as disciples of Christ.*

## To Help You
# REMEMBER

**1.** God commands us to be people of truth and integrity.

**2.** If we lie or covet another's goods, we are to make amends.

**3.** On our journey to Heaven, we are to form humble and generous hearts.

**WITH MY FAMILY**

Discuss with your family the following question, "What one thing does our family most seek in life? Why?"

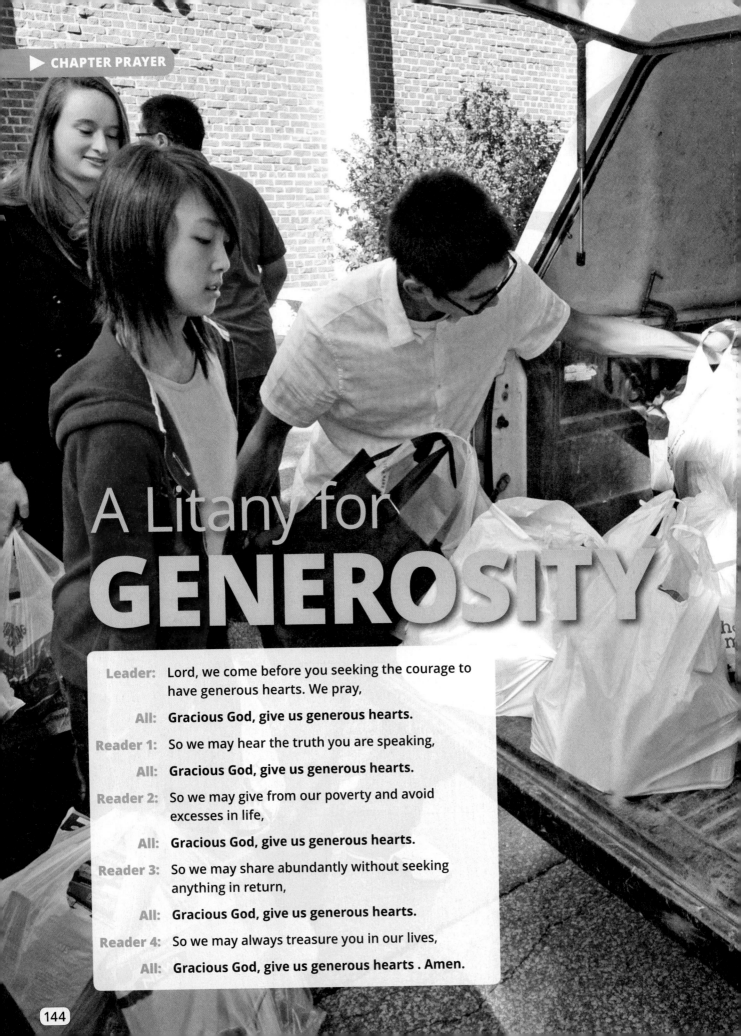

# A Litany for
# GENEROSITY

**Leader:** Lord, we come before you seeking the courage to have generous hearts. We pray,

**All:** **Gracious God, give us generous hearts.**

**Reader 1:** So we may hear the truth you are speaking,

**All:** **Gracious God, give us generous hearts.**

**Reader 2:** So we may give from our poverty and avoid excesses in life,

**All:** **Gracious God, give us generous hearts.**

**Reader 3:** So we may share abundantly without seeking anything in return,

**All:** **Gracious God, give us generous hearts.**

**Reader 4:** So we may always treasure you in our lives,

**All:** **Gracious God, give us generous hearts . Amen.**

**LOOKING AHEAD**
In this chapter the Holy
Spirit invites you to ▶

**EXPLORE** those who embody the Gospel.
**DISCOVER** the meaning of the Lord's Prayer.
**DECIDE** how to put prayer into action.

CHAPTER **12**

# The Lord's Prayer

▶ **What plans do you have for the future?**

Architects draw up plans and blueprints that
detail the structures they intend to build.
Jesus gave us a blueprint for building our lives
when he taught his disciples the Lord's Prayer.

*"This is how you are to pray: Our Father in
heaven: . . ."*
                                    MATTHEW: 6:9

▶ **Why do you think Christians pray the
Lord's Prayer every day?**

**TIMELINE**

| | | |
|---|---|---|
| **1194–1253** Life of St. Clare of Assisi | **1260** Construction on Basilicia di Santa Clare begins. | **1559** Book of Common Prayer in English is published. |

**1150**          **1450**          **1750**          **2050**

**1212–1250**
Reign of Frederick II, Holy Roman Emperor

**1962**
US Supreme Court rules in *Engel v. Vitale*.

145

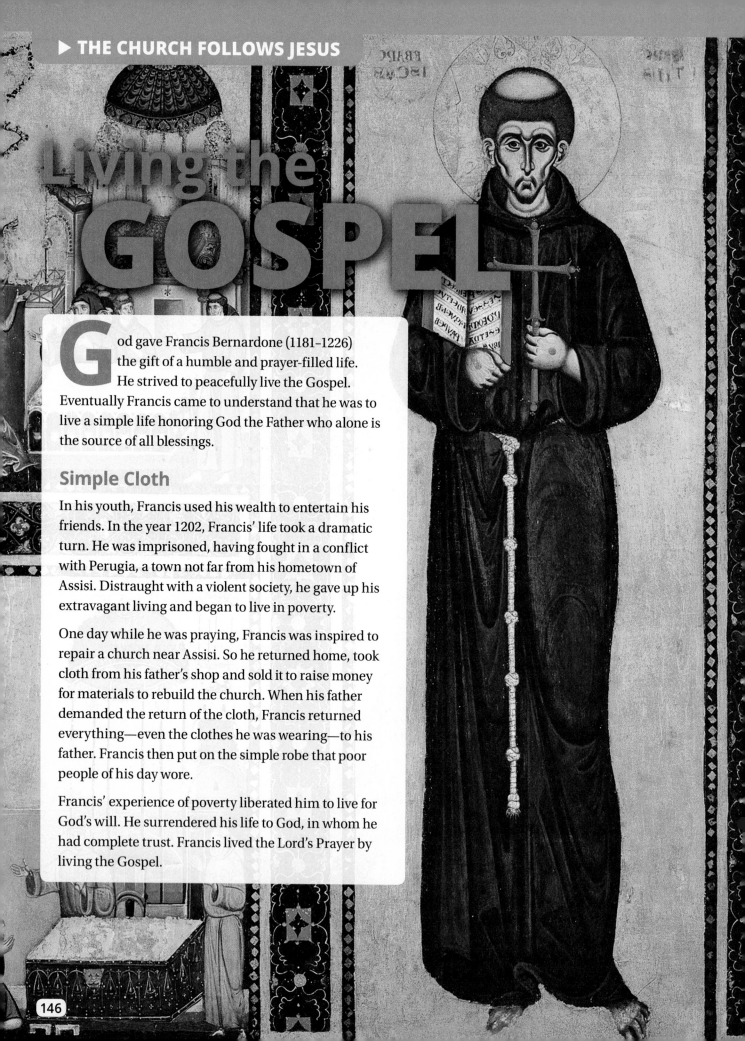

# Living the GOSPEL

**G**od gave Francis Bernardone (1181–1226) the gift of a humble and prayer-filled life. He strived to peacefully live the Gospel. Eventually Francis came to understand that he was to live a simple life honoring God the Father who alone is the source of all blessings.

## Simple Cloth

In his youth, Francis used his wealth to entertain his friends. In the year 1202, Francis' life took a dramatic turn. He was imprisoned, having fought in a conflict with Perugia, a town not far from his hometown of Assisi. Distraught with a violent society, he gave up his extravagant living and began to live in poverty.

One day while he was praying, Francis was inspired to repair a church near Assisi. So he returned home, took cloth from his father's shop and sold it to raise money for materials to rebuild the church. When his father demanded the return of the cloth, Francis returned everything—even the clothes he was wearing—to his father. Francis then put on the simple robe that poor people of his day wore.

Francis' experience of poverty liberated him to live for God's will. He surrendered his life to God, in whom he had complete trust. Francis lived the Lord's Prayer by living the Gospel.

## Devoted to God

Clare was like Francis. She had been raised in a wealthy family in Assisi. Clare developed a love for the poor early in her life. When her parents tried to marry her to a wealthy Italian nobleman, she ran away and joined up with Francis, who welcomed her in his work. Like Francis, she was utterly dedicated to poverty as a way to show her absolute dependence on God and his will.

Both Francis and Clare depended completely on the generosity of others, begging for their "daily bread." Unlike Francis and his friars, Clare was unable to roam the countryside because it was unsafe for a woman to do so in that time. She and her sister, Agnes, founded a group of women who focused on prayer, fasting and good works. They stayed near San Damiano Church in Assisi, the church that Francis had restored.

▶ **What do you think begging for what you need might be like?**

A number of miracles were attributed to Clare during her lifetime, and her devotion and holiness was widely known. On one occasion, it was said that she held off the soldiers of Emperor Frederick II by kneeling with the Blessed Sacrament at the gates of her monastery.

Francis was canonized in 1228, just two years after his death. Clare was canonized as a Saint in 1255, only two years after her death. The Franciscan Order and the Order of Poor Clares still continue their work today.

## Disciple POWER

**PRAYER**
There are many ways to pray, but a Christian cannot live without prayer. Prayer is our lifeline to God. Prayer reminds us that we are called not only to do good, but to have a personal relationship with God on a daily basis.

## FAITH JOURNAL

Why would a life of poverty or simplicity be beneficial for your relationship with God?

## Summary of the Gospel

The Lord's Prayer helps make the Gospel come alive in our lives. Jesus, the architect of the Gospel, gave this prayer to his followers so they would have a blueprint on how to live the Gospel. Jesus taught that the Christian life is built on prayer and has at its center a relationship with God.

The Lord's Prayer, or the Our Father, is a summary of the Gospel. The Christian writer Tertullian (ca. 160–225) described the Lord's Prayer as "the summary of the whole Gospel." Later Saint Augustine of Hippo (354–430) wrote: "Run through all the words of the holy prayers [in Scripture] and I do not think that you will find anything in them that is not contained and included in the Lord's Prayer."

Jesus, the master and model of prayer, taught us to pray the Our Father. Flowing from Jesus' heart, this prayer expresses the intimacy between Jesus and his Father. By giving us this prayer, Jesus invites us to share in that intimacy. And so in this way we can nurture our relationship with God as his children.

## Teaching to Pray

The Lord's Prayer is part of the Sermon on the Mount in Matthew's account of the Gospel. Jesus said:

> "This is how you are to pray:
> Our Father in heaven,
>     hallowed be your name,
>         your kingdom come,
>     your will be done,
>         on earth as in heaven.
> Give us today our daily bread;
> and forgive us our debts,
> as we forgive our debtors;
> and do not subject us to the
>     final test,
> but deliver us from the evil one."

MATTHEW 6: 9–13

▶ In what ways does the Lord's Prayer nurture your relationship with God?

# A Blueprint for LIVING

## A Plan of Prayer

Having just taught the Lord's Prayer, Jesus concludes:

*"If you forgive others their transgressions, your heavenly Father will forgive you. But if you do not forgive others, neither will your Father forgive your transgressions."*

MATTHEW 6:14–15

On the surface, the words of the Lord's Prayer are simple enough. But there is sufficient sustenance here to provide us food for a lifetime of meditation. The first half of the Lord's Prayer describes our belief in God and his plan for us. The second half presents our needs to God.

From this, we can understand how the Lord's Prayer is a blueprint for living the Gospel. So by faith we respond in prayer to the love God has for us and for all people.

## Faith **CONNECTION**

In small groups, describe gestures you can include in praying the Lord's Prayer.

**Our Father** _____

**hallowed be thy name** _____

**thy kingdom come** _____

**thy will . . . in heaven** _____

**Give us our daily bread** _____

**forgive us . . .** _____

**as we forgive . . .** _____

**lead us not into temptation** _____

**deliver us from evil.** _____

## Our Father in Heaven

The first words we speak in a conversation are always important. These words set the tone for the remainder of the conversation. The very first words of the Lord's Prayer set the tone for our conversation with God in prayer. We pray "Our Father, who art in heaven, . . ."

God is our loving, caring, faithful Father. His love for us has no limits. God is the Father of everyone. He is the God of Heaven and Earth, the Almighty One, the Creator. He has entered into a covenant of friendship with his people.

▶ Why is it correct to call God our Father?

## Hallowed Be Thy Name

After addressing God as Father, we pray seven petitions. The first three petitions focus on God and acknowledge that God is the center of our lives. The final four petitions acknowledge our dependence on God for our every need and our very lives.

In the first petition, we acknowledge the goodness and holiness of God. God is so good that we describe his very name as holy. The word *hallowed* means "holy." God created us to share in his holiness. We are to live holy lives. In Jesus' final prayer for his disciples, he prayed:

> *"Holy Father, keep them in your name that you have given me, so that they may be one just as we are."* JOHN **17:11**

With the birth of the Church, we experience the overwhelming goodness and holiness of God in prayer, the celebration of the Seven Sacraments, and in the example and witness of believers as they live the Catholic faith.

▶ In what ways do you experience God's holiness on a daily basis?

## Thy Kingdom Come

At the heart of Jesus' preaching is the announcement of the coming of the Kingdom of God. The kingdom is the right relationship between God and his people, and his people with one another. In God's kingdom peace, justice, mercy, forgiveness, love, and friendship abound. There will be no more hunger, no more war, no more hatred and bigotry, and ignorance. In light of all that, Lord, thy kingdom come! We believe and hope that the kingdom will come when Christ returns in glory.

## Thy Will Be Done

If God's kingdom is the kingdom of love, peace and justice, then indeed God truly wills these things. When we pray "Thy will be done on earth," we are committing ourselves to be instruments of God's kingdom. His will begins with each of us. Each day, we pray the Lord's Prayer to recommit ourselves to stay focused. This is at the heart of why God created us— to be open to his will in our lives and to obediently act in faith.

God's will is that his loving plan of creation and Salvation be brought to completion. In this third petition, we affirm not only that God loves us, cares for us, and has a plan for us; we also affirm that we will live in such a way as to work at bringing about God's will, his plan, his kingdom.

▶ What might you do to better prepare for the coming of the kingdom?

## Our Daily Bread

The beauty of this petition is in its simplicity. We only need our "daily bread." We need only that which brings us life. Jesus taught us:

*"What father among you would hand his son a snake when he asks for a fish? . . . [H]ow much more will the Father in heaven give The holy Spirit to those who ask him?"* Luke 11:11, 13

With trust and confidence we place our spiritual and material needs ("our daily bread") before God. We not only talk to God about ourselves; we also pray with and for one another. In a world where so many people go hungry, God can use each of us to bring that "daily bread" to those most in need.

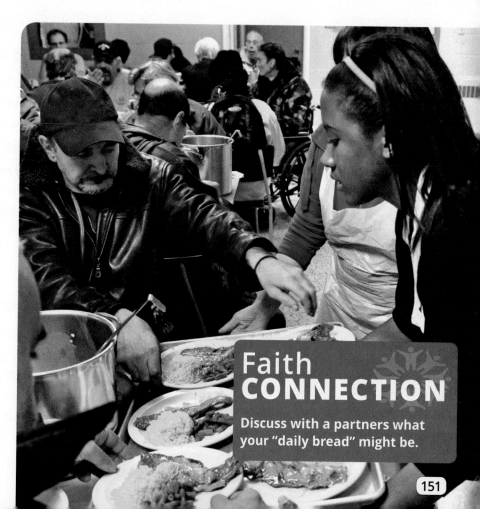

## Faith CONNECTION

Discuss with a partners what your "daily bread" might be.

## Forgive Us . . . as We Forgive

In this petition, we acknowledge that we sometimes turn our hearts away from God's love. We sin. We are in need of God's forgiveness. And we are to ask God to forgive us "as we forgive those who trespass against us." In other words, we cannot just keep asking God for forgiveness without changing our own hearts. We too must become people of forgiveness as well. God will forgive everything that needs forgiving if we are truly sorry. Jesus said:

> *"If you forgive others their transgressions, your heavenly Father will forgive you. But if you do not forgive others, neither will your Father forgive your transgressions."*
> MATTHEW 6:14–15

## Lead Us Not into Temptation

Jesus was tempted. Yet he said "no" to the temptations and "yes" to the will of His Father. **Temptation** is all that moves us away from holiness. In this petition, we ask for the guidance of the Holy Spirit to see the truth in every situation and to recognize evil for the lie that it is.

So of course, God does not *lead us into temptation*. This petition is asking for the grace to *keep ourselves* away from temptation. And we trust that God will give us the strength to do so.

## Deliver Us from Evil

At the Last Supper Jesus said:

> *"I do not ask that you take them out of the world but that you keep them from the evil one."*
> JOHN 17:15

Satan is the "evil one" from whom Jesus asks us to be delivered. Filled with the Holy Spirit, we confidently share our deepest hopes with God our Father. We pray and hope that we will share now and forever in the victory of Jesus Christ over evil and death.

# DEPENDING ON PRAYER

**There is a saying,** "You cannot give what you do not have." This is true for faith and prayer. Faith needs prayer, and prayer depends on faith.

## FORMS OF PRAYER

**The Church teaches us that there are five forms of prayer.** We use all of these forms of prayer in the liturgy:

- **Blessing and Adoration.** This form of prayer declares and acknowledges that God is the Creator and we are his creatures. God is the source of all that is good. We bless and adore God who created everything and everyone.

- **Petition.** A prayer of petition asks God to give us the help we need in our daily lives. We trust God to provide for us, to give us what we need.

- **Intercession.** This form of prayer helps us become aware of the needs of others. We ask God to bless, heal, or take care of those who are in need of his help and guidance.

- **Thanksgiving.** Being thankful is synonymous with being a disciple of Christ. Saint Paul teaches us that we are to give thanks in every circumstance (read 1 Thessalonians 5:18).

- **Praise.** Our prayer of praise acknowledges that God is God. We are to give glory to God simply because he is God.

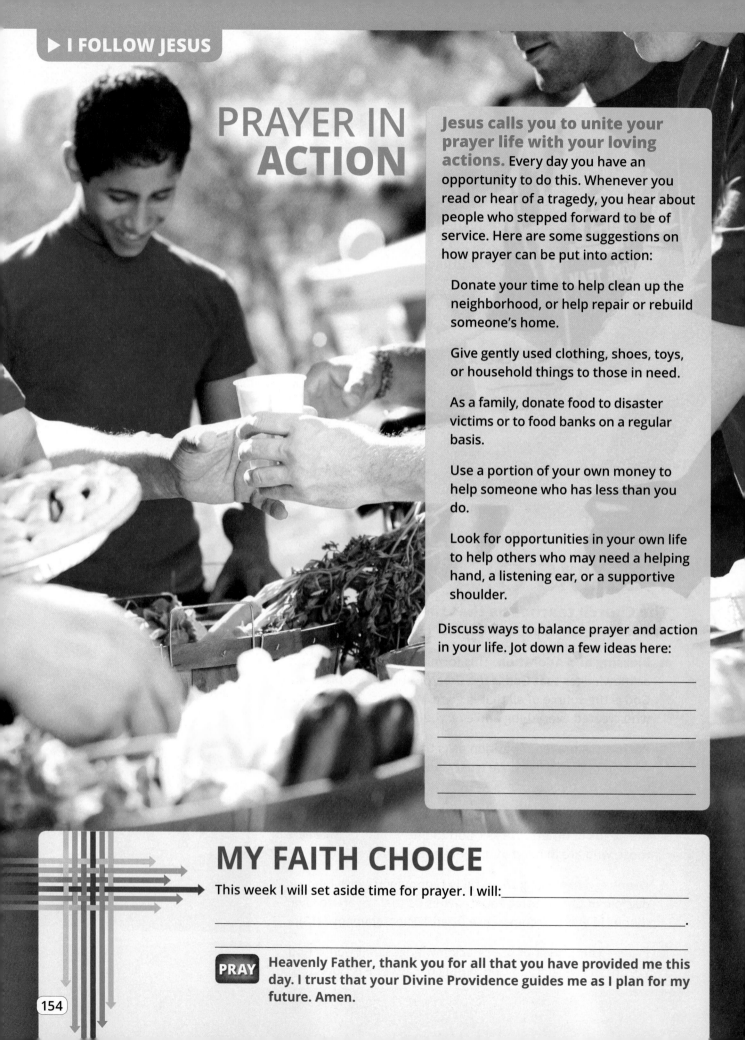

# PRAYER IN ACTION

**Jesus calls you to unite your prayer life with your loving actions.** Every day you have an opportunity to do this. Whenever you read or hear of a tragedy, you hear about people who stepped forward to be of service. Here are some suggestions on how prayer can be put into action:

Donate your time to help clean up the neighborhood, or help repair or rebuild someone's home.

Give gently used clothing, shoes, toys, or household things to those in need.

As a family, donate food to disaster victims or to food banks on a regular basis.

Use a portion of your own money to help someone who has less than you do.

Look for opportunities in your own life to help others who may need a helping hand, a listening ear, or a supportive shoulder.

Discuss ways to balance prayer and action in your life. Jot down a few ideas here:

_____

_____

_____

_____

_____

# MY FAITH CHOICE

This week I will set aside time for prayer. I will:_____

_____.

_____

**PRAY** Heavenly Father, thank you for all that you have provided me this day. I trust that your Divine Providence guides me as I plan for my future. Amen.

## Recall

*Define each of these faith terms:*

**1.** hallowed _____

**2.** Kingdom of God _____

**3.** temptation _____

*Choose two of the following questions to answer. Write a brief response to answer each of your choices.*

**4.** Explain how the Lord's Prayer encourages us to trust in God's forgiveness.

_____

_____

**5.** Describe the focus of the first three petitions of the Lord's Prayer.

_____

_____

**6.** Describe the focus of the final four petitions of the Lord's Prayer.

_____

_____

### To Help You REMEMBER

**1.** The Lord's Prayer is the one prayer that Jesus taught his disciples to pray.

**2.** At the heart of the prayer is an understanding of God as Father.

**3.** The Lord's Prayer contains many key points about God's kingdom.

## Reflect

*Using what you have learned in this chapter, briefly explain this statement:*

> You cannot call the God of all kindness your Father if you preserve a cruel and inhuman heart.
>
> SAINT JOHN CHRYSOSTOM

_____

_____

## Share

*Discuss in a small group the Lord's Prayer as a blueprint for Christian living.*

## WITH MY FAMILY

Since we ask God to "give us this day our daily bread," we too must do the same for one another. Discuss with your family the question, "What daily bread do we need to share with one another?"

# The Lord's Prayer

**Leader:** Let us pray as Jesus taught us:

**All:** Our Father, who art in heaven, hallowed be thy name;

**Group 1:** thy kingdom come, thy will be done on earth as it is in heaven.

**Group 2:** Give us this day our daily bread, and forgive us our trespasses,

**All:** as we forgive those who trespass against us; and lead us not into temptation, but deliver us from evil. Amen.

## A Choose the Best Word

*Answer each question by circling the best answer.*

**1.** As a result of the Second Vatican Council, the Church focused more on doing what?

A. responding to the challenges of the modern world

B. reading the signs of the times and interpreting them in light of the Gospel

C. seeking for continual inner renewal to better transform the world

D. all of the above

**2.** What does it mean to keep holy the Lord's Day?

A. honoring God only on the third day of every week

B. keeping Sunday as a day set aside to worship God and recreate our relationship with him

C. preserving one day a week to have restful sleep

D. remembering to go to church once a month

**3.** Which of the following is an example of keeping the Fifth Commandment?

A. abortion

B. respecting life

C. euthanasia

D. taking illegal drugs

**4.** Placing an intimate sexual relationship only within a lifelong marriage is in accordance with which of the Ten Commandments?

A. the Fifth Commandment

B. the Sixth Commandment

C. the Seventh Commandment

D. none of the above

**5.** Which of the Ten Commandments is related to stewardship, that is, our call to responsibly manage and care for all of God's creation?

A. the Fifth Commandment

B. the Sixth Commandment

C. the Seventh Commandment

D. none of the above

## B Show What You Know

*Match the item in Column A with those in Column B.*

**Column A**

_____ 1. temptation

_____ 2. direct abortion

_____ 3. greed

_____ 4. reparation

_____ 5. lying

_____ 6. avarice

_____ 7. euthanasia

_____ 8. chastity

_____ 9. perjury

_____ 10. hedonism

**Column B**

A. appropriately integrating the gift of sexuality within oneself in accord with God's plan for life and love

B. intentional killing of an unborn child

C. killing of a person suffering from a long-term illness

D. to pay for misdeeds

E. intentionally deceiving another person

F. excessive passion for wealth and power

G. unchecked desire to have more and more

H. a lure to do evil or sin

I. lying under oath

J. placing pleasure above all else

## C Connect with Scripture

*Reread the Scripture passage on the first Unit Opener page. What connection do you see between this passage and what you learned in this unit?*

_____

_____

_____

## D Be a Disciple

1. *Review The Church Follows Jesus in each of the chapters. Which person or ministry of the Church has inspired you to be a better disciple of Jesus? Explain your response.*

_____

_____

_____

2. *Work with a group. Review the six Disciple Power habits you have learned about in this unit. After jotting down your own ideas, share with the group practical ways that you will live these day by day.*

_____

_____

_____

# CATHOLIC PRAYERS and PRACTICES

## Sign of the Cross

In the name of the Father,
and of the Son,
and of the Holy Spirit. Amen.

## Signum Crucis

In nómine Patris,
et Fílii,
et Spíritus Sancti. Amen.

## Our Father

Our Father, who art in heaven,
hallowed be thy name;
thy kingdom come,
thy will be done
on earth as it is in heaven.
Give us this day our daily bread,
and forgive us our trespasses,
as we forgive those who trespass
    against us;
and lead us not into temptation
    but deliver us from evil.
Amen.

## Pater Noster

Pater noster, qui es in cælis:
sanctificétur nomen tuum;
advéniat regnum tuum;
fiat volúntas tua, sicut in cælo,
    et in terra.
Panem nostrum cotidiánum
    da nobis hódie;
et dimítte nobis débita nostra,
sicut et nos dimíttimus
    debitóribus nostris;
et ne nos indúcas in tentatiónem;
sed líbera nos a malo. Amen.

## Glory Be (Doxology)

Glory be to the Father
and to the Son
and to the Holy Spirit,
as it was in the beginning
is now, and ever shall be
world without end. Amen.

## Gloria Patri

Glória Patri
et Fílio
et Spirítui Sancto.
Sicut erat in princípio,
et nunc et semper
et in sǽcula sæculórum. Amen.

## The Hail Mary

Hail, Mary, full of grace,
the Lord is with thee.
Blessed art thou among women
and blessed is the fruit of thy
    womb, Jesus.
Holy Mary, Mother of God,
pray for us sinners,
now and at the hour of our death.
Amen.

## Ave, Maria

Ave, María, grátia plena,
Dóminus tecum.
Benedícta tu in muliéribus,
et benedíctus fructus ventris tui, Iesus.
Sancta María, Mater Dei,
ora pro nobis peccatóribus,
nunc et in hora mortis nostræ.
Amen.

# Apostles' Creed

(from the *Roman Missal*)

I believe in God,
the Father almighty,
Creator of heaven and earth,
and in Jesus Christ, his only Son, our Lord,

*(At the words that follow, up to and
including the Virgin Mary, all bow.)*

who was conceived by the Holy Spirit,
born of the Virgin Mary,
suffered under Pontius Pilate,
was crucified, died and was buried;
he descended into hell;
on the third day he rose again from the dead;
he ascended into heaven,
and is seated at the right hand of God the Father almighty;
from there he will come to judge the living and the dead.

I believe in the Holy Spirit,
the holy catholic Church,
the communion of saints,
the forgiveness of sins,
the resurrection of the body,
and life everlasting. Amen.

# Nicene Creed

(from the *Roman Missal*)

I believe in one God,
the Father almighty,
maker of heaven and earth,
of all things visible and invisible.

I believe in one Lord Jesus Christ,
the Only Begotten Son of God,
born of the Father before all ages.
God from God, Light from Light,
true God from true God,
begotten, not made, consubstantial with the Father;
through him all things were made.
For us men and for our salvation
he came down from heaven,

*(At the words that follow, up to and
including and became man, all bow.)*

and by the Holy Spirit was incarnate of the Virgin Mary,
and became man.

For our sake he was crucified under Pontius Pilate,
he suffered death and was buried,
and rose again on the third day
in accordance with the Scriptures.
He ascended into heaven
and is seated at the right hand of the Father.
He will come again in glory
to judge the living and the dead
and his kingdom will have no end.

I believe in the Holy Spirit, the Lord, the giver of life,
who proceeds from the Father and the Son,
who with the Father and the Son is adored and glorified,
who has spoken through the prophets.

I believe in one, holy, catholic and apostolic Church.
I confess one Baptism for the forgiveness of sins
and I look forward to the resurrection of the dead
and the life of the world to come. Amen.

# Morning Prayer

Dear God,
as I begin this day,
keep me in your love and care.
Help me to live as your child today.
Bless me, my family, and my friends
    in all we do.
Keep us all close to you. Amen.

# Grace Before Meals

Bless us, O Lord,
and these thy gifts,
which we are about to receive
from thy bounty,
through Christ our Lord.
Amen.

# Grace After Meals

We give thee thanks,
for all thy benefits, almighty God,
who lives and reigns forever.
Amen.

# Evening Prayer

Dear God,
I thank you for today.
Keep me safe throughout the night.
Thank you for all the good I did today.
I am sorry for what I have chosen
    to do wrong.
Bless my family and friends. Amen.

# A Vocation Prayer

God, I know you will call me
for special work in my life.
Help me follow Jesus each day
and be ready to answer your call. Amen.

# Prayer to the Holy Spirit

Come, Holy Spirit, fill the hearts
    of your faithful.
And kindle in them the
    fire of your love.
Send forth your Spirit and
    they shall be created.
And you will renew the
    face of the earth. Amen.

# Act of Contrition

My God,
I am sorry for my sins
    with all my heart.
In choosing to do wrong
and failing to do good,
I have sinned against you
whom I should love above all things.
I firmly intend, with your help,
to do penance,
to sin no more,
and to avoid whatever leads me to sin.
Our Savior Jesus Christ
suffered and died for us.
In his name, my God, have mercy. Amen.

## The Beatitudes

"Blessed are the poor in spirit,
　for theirs is the kingdom of heaven.
Blessed are they who mourn,
　for they will be comforted.
Blessed are the meek,
　for they will inherit the land.
Blessed are they who hunger
　　and thirst for righteousness,
　for they will be satisfied.
Blessed are the merciful,
　for they will be shown mercy.
Blessed are the clean of heart,
　for they will see God.
Blessed are the peacemakers,
　for they will be called children of God
Blessed are they who are persecuted for
　　the sake of righteousness,
　for theirs is the kingdom of heaven."

Matthew 5:3–10

## The Angelus

Leader: The Angel of the Lord declared unto Mary,

Response: And she conceived of the Holy Spirit.

All: **Hail, Mary . . .**

Leader: Behold the handmaid of the Lord,

Response: Be it done unto me according to your Word.

All: **Hail, Mary . . .**

Leader: And the Word was made flesh

Response: And dwelt among us.

All: **Hail, Mary . . .**

Leader: Pray for us, O holy Mother of God,

Response: That we may be made worthy of the promises of Christ.

Leader: Let us pray. Pour forth, we beseech you, O Lord, your grace into our hearts: that we, to whom the Incarnation of Christ your Son was made known by the message of an Angel, may by his Passion and Cross be brought to the glory of his Resurrection. Through the same Christ our Lord. Amen.

All: **Amen.**

# The Ten Commandments

1. I am the LORD your God: you shall not have strange gods before me.

2. You shall not take the name of the LORD your God in vain.

3. Remember to keep holy the LORD's Day.

4. Honor your father and your mother.

5. You shall not kill.

6. You shall not commit adultery.

7. You shall not steal.

8. You shall not lie.

9. You shall not covet your neighbor's wife.

10. You shall not covet your neighbor's goods.

Based on Exodus 20:2–3, 7–17

# Precepts of the Church

1. Participate in Mass on Sundays and holy days of obligation, and rest from unnecessary work.

2. Confess sins at least once a year.

3. Receive Holy Communion at least during the Easter season.

4. Observe the prescribed days of fasting and abstinence.

5. Provide for the material needs of the Church, according to one's abilities.

# The Great Commandment

"You shall love the Lord, your God, with all your heart, with all your soul, and with all your mind. . . . You shall love your neighbor as yourself."

Matthew 22:37, 39

# The Law of Love

"This is my commandment: love one another as I love you."

John 15:12

# Corporal Works of Mercy

Feed people who are hungry.
Give drink to people who are thirsty.
Clothe people who need clothes.
Visit people who are in prison.
Shelter people who are homeless.
Visit people who are sick.
Bury people who have died.

# Spiritual Works of Mercy

Help people who sin.
Teach people who are ignorant.
Give advice to people who have doubts.
Comfort people who suffer.
Be patient with other people.
Forgive people who hurt you.
Pray for people who are alive and for those who have died.

# Rosary

Catholics pray the Rosary to honor Mary and remember the important events in the life of Jesus and Mary. There are twenty mysteries of the Rosary. Follow the steps from 1 to 5.

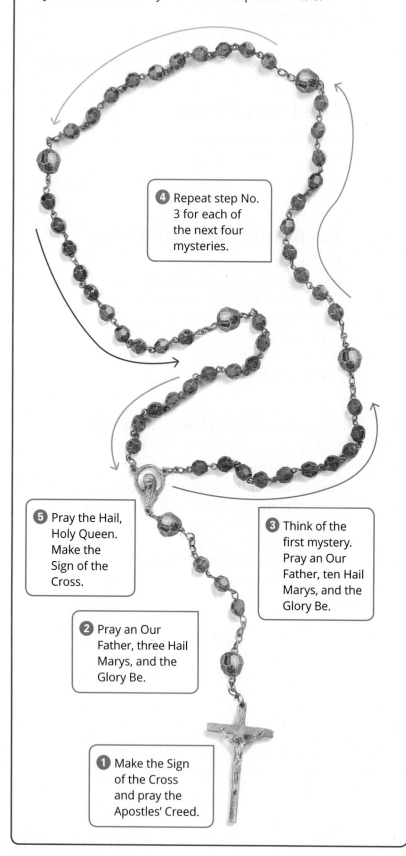

**4** Repeat step No. 3 for each of the next four mysteries.

**5** Pray the Hail, Holy Queen. Make the Sign of the Cross.

**3** Think of the first mystery. Pray an Our Father, ten Hail Marys, and the Glory Be.

**2** Pray an Our Father, three Hail Marys, and the Glory Be.

**1** Make the Sign of the Cross and pray the Apostles' Creed.

## Joyful Mysteries

**1** The Annunciation
**2** The Visitation
**3** The Nativity
**4** The Presentation in the Temple
**5** The Finding of the Child Jesus After Three Days in the Temple

## Luminous Mysteries

**1** The Baptism at the Jordan
**2** The Miracle at Cana
**3** The Proclamation of the Kingdom and the Call to Conversation
**4** The Transfiguration
**5** The Institution of the Eucharist

## Sorrowful Mysteries

**1** The Agony in the Garden
**2** The Scourging at the Pillar
**3** The Crowning with Thorns
**4** The Carrying of the Cross
**5** The Crucifixion and Death

## Glorious Mysteries

**1** The Resurrection
**2** The Ascension
**3** The Descent of the Holy Spirit at Pentecost
**4** The Assumption of Mary
**5** The Crowning of the Blessed Virgin as Queen of Heaven and Earth

## Hail, Holy Queen

Hail, holy Queen, Mother of mercy:
Hail, our life, our sweetness
        and our hope.
To you do we cry, poor banished
        children of Eve.
To you do we send up our sighs,
mourning and weeping
        in this valley of tears.
Turn then, most gracious advocate,
your eyes of mercy toward us;
and after this our exile
show unto us the blessed fruit
        of your womb, Jesus.
O clement, O loving, O sweet
        Virgin Mary.

# Stations of the Cross

**1.** Jesus is condemned to death.

**2.** Jesus accepts his cross.

**3.** Jesus falls the first time.

**4.** Jesus meets his mother.

**5.** Simon helps Jesus carry the cross.

**6.** Veronica wipes the face of Jesus.

**7.** Jesus falls the second time.

**8.** Jesus meets the women of Jerusalem.

**9.** Jesus falls the third time.

**10.** Jesus is stripped of his clothes.

**11.** Jesus is nailed to the cross.

**12.** Jesus dies on the cross.

**13.** Jesus is taken down from the cross.

**14.** Jesus is buried in the tomb.

(Some parishes conclude the Stations by reflecting on the Resurrection of Jesus.)

# WE CELEBRATE the MASS

## The Introductory Rites

We remember that we are the community of the Church.
We prepare to listen to the Word of God and to celebrate the Eucharist.

### The Entrance

We stand as the priest, deacon, and other ministers enter the assembly. We sing a gathering song. The priest and deacon kiss the altar. The priest then goes to the chair where he presides over the celebration.

### Greeting of the Altar and of the People Gathered

The priest leads us in praying the Sign of the Cross. The priest greets us, and we say,
   **"And with your spirit."**

### The Penitential Act

We admit our wrongdoings.
We bless God for his mercy.

### The Gloria

We praise God for all the good that he has done for us.

### The Collect

The priest leads us in praying the Collect. We respond,
**"Amen."**

## The Liturgy of the Word

God speaks to us today. We listen and respond to God's Word.

### The First Reading from Scripture

We sit and listen as the lector reads from the Old Testament or from the Acts of the Apostles. The lector concludes, "The word of the Lord." We respond,
   **"Thanks be to God."**

### The Responsorial Psalm

The cantor leads us in singing a psalm.

### The Second Reading from Scripture

The lector reads from the New Testament, but not from the four Gospels. The lector concludes, "The word of the Lord." We respond,
   **"Thanks be to God."**

### The Acclamation

We stand to honor Christ, present with us in the Gospel. The song leader leads us in singing **"Alleluia, Alleluia, Alleluia,"** or another acclamation during Lent.

### The Gospel

The deacon or priest proclaims, "A reading from the holy Gospel according to (name of Gospel writer)." We respond,
   **"Glory to you, O Lord."**
He proclaims the Gospel. At the end he says, "The Gospel of the Lord."
We respond,
   **"Praise to you, Lord Jesus Christ."**

## The Homily

We sit. The priest or deacon preaches the homily. He helps the people gathered to understand the Word of God spoken to us in the readings.

## The Profession of Faith

We stand and profess our faith.
We pray the Nicene Creed or the Apostles' Creed together.

## The Prayer of the Faithful

The priest leads us in praying for our Church and her leaders, for our country and its leaders, for ourselves and others, for those who are sick and those who have died. We can respond to each prayer in several ways. One way that we respond is,

**"Lord, hear our prayer."**

# The Liturgy of the Eucharist

We join with Jesus and the Holy Spirit to give thanks and praise to God the Father.

## The Preparation of the Altar and Gifts

We sit as the altar is prepared and the collection is taken up. We share our blessings with the community of the Church and especially with those in need. The song leader may lead us in singing a song. The gifts of bread and wine are brought to the altar.

The priest lifts up the bread and blesses God for all our gifts. He prays, "Blessed are you, Lord God of all creation . . ." We respond,

**"Blessed be God for ever."**

The priest lifts up the cup of wine and prays, "Blessed are you, Lord God of all creation . . . "
We respond,

**"Blessed be God for ever."**

The priest invites us,
"Pray, brothers and sisters, that my sacrifice and yours may be acceptable to God, the almighty Father."

We stand and respond,

**"May the Lord accept the sacrifice at your hands for the praise and glory of his name, for our good, and the good of all his holy Church."**

## The Prayer over the Offerings

The priest leads us in praying the Prayer over the Offerings.
We respond, **"Amen."**

## Preface

The priest invites us to join in praying the Church's great prayer of praise and thanksgiving to God the Father.

| | |
|---|---|
| **Priest:** | "The Lord be with you." |
| **Assembly:** | **"And with your spirit."** |
| **Priest:** | "Lift up your hearts." |
| **Assembly:** | **"We lift them up to the Lord."** |
| **Priest:** | "Let us give thanks to the Lord our God." |
| **Assembly:** | **"It is right and just."** |

After the priest sings or prays aloud the Preface, we join in acclaiming,

**"Holy, Holy, Holy Lord God of hosts.
Heaven and earth are full of your glory.
Hosanna in the highest.
Blessed is he who comes in the name of the Lord.
Hosanna in the highest."**

## The Eucharistic Prayer

The priest leads the assembly in praying the Eucharistic Prayer. We call on the Holy Spirit to make our gifts of bread and wine holy and that they become the Body and Blood of Jesus. We recall what happened at the Last Supper. The bread and wine become the Body and Blood of the Lord. Jesus is truly and really present under the appearances of bread and wine.

The priest sings or says aloud, "The mystery of faith." We respond using this or another acclamation used by the Church,

**"We proclaim your Death, O Lord, and profess your Resurrection until you come again."**

The priest then prays for the Church. He prays for the living and the dead.

## Doxology

The priest concludes the praying of the Eucharistic Prayer. He sings or prays aloud,

"Through him, and with him, and in him,
O God, almighty Father,
in the unity of the Holy Spirit,
all glory and honor is yours,
for ever and ever."

We respond by singing, **"Amen."**

# The Communion Rite

## The Lord's Prayer

We pray the Lord's Prayer together.

## The Sign of Peace

The priest invites us to share a sign of peace, saying, "The peace of the Lord be with you always." We respond,

**"And with your spirit."**

We share a sign of peace.

## The Fraction, or the Breaking of the Bread

The priest breaks the host, the consecrated bread. We sing or pray aloud,

**"Lamb of God, you take away
the sins of the world,
have mercy on us.
Lamb of God, you take away
the sins of the world,
have mercy on us.
Lamb of God, you take away
the sins of the world,
grant us peace."**

## Communion

The priest raises the host and says aloud,

"Behold the Lamb of God,
behold him who takes away the sins
of the world.
Blessed are those called to the supper
of the Lamb."

We join with him and say,

**"Lord, I am not worthy
that you should enter under my roof,
but only say the word
and my soul shall be healed."**

The priest receives Communion. Next, the deacon and the extraordinary ministers of Holy Communion and the members of the assembly receive Communion.

The priest, deacon, or extraordinary minister of Holy Communion holds up the host. We bow, and the priest, deacon, or extraordinary minister of Holy Communion says, "The Body of Christ." We respond, **"Amen."** We then receive the consecrated host in our hands or on our tongues.

If we are to receive the Blood of Christ, the priest, deacon, or extraordinary minister of Holy Communion holds up the cup containing the consecrated wine. We bow, and the priest, deacon, or extraordinary minister of Holy Communion says, "The Blood of Christ." We respond, **"Amen."** We take the cup in our hands and drink from it.

## The Prayer after Communion

We stand as the priest invites us to pray, saying, "Let us pray." He prays the Prayer after Communion. We respond,
**"Amen."**

# The Concluding Rites

We are sent forth to do good works, praising and blessing the Lord.

## Greeting

We stand. The priest greets us as we prepare to leave. He says, "The Lord be with you."
We respond,
> **"And with your spirit."**

## Final Blessing

The priest or deacon may invite us,
> "Bow down for the blessing."

The priest blesses us, saying,
> May almighty God bless you,
> the Father, and the Son,
> and the Holy Spirit."
We respond, **"Amen."**

## Dismissal of the People

The priest or deacon sends us forth, using these or similar words,
> "Go in peace, glorifying the Lord
> by your life."
We respond,
> **"Thanks be to God."**

We sing a hymn. The priest and the deacon kiss the altar. The priest, deacon, and other ministers bow to the altar and leave in procession.

# KEY TEACHINGS of the CHURCH

## DIVINE REVELATION

### Who am I?
Every human person has been created by God to live in friendship with him both here on Earth and forever in Heaven.

### How do we know this about ourselves?
We know this because every human person desires to know and love God and wants God to know and love them. We also know this because God told us this about ourselves and about him.

### How did God tell us?
First of all God tells us this through creation, which is the work of God; creation reflects the goodness and beauty of the Creator and tells us about God the Creator. Secondly, God came to us and told us, or revealed this about himself. He revealed this most fully by sending his Son, Jesus Christ, who became one of us and lived among us.

### What is faith?
Faith is a supernatural gift from God that enables us to know God and all that he has revealed, and to respond to God with our whole heart and mind.

### What is a mystery of faith?
The word *mystery* describes the fact that we can never fully comprehend or fully grasp God and his loving plan for us. We only know who God is and his plan for us through Divine Revelation.

### What is Divine Revelation?
Divine Revelation is God's free gift of making himself known to us and giving himself to us by gradually communicating in deeds and words his own mystery and his divine plan for humanity. God reveals himself so that we can live in communion with him and with one another forever.

### What is Sacred Tradition?
The word *tradition* comes from a Latin word meaning "to pass on." Sacred Tradition is the passing on of Divine Revelation by the Church through the power and guidance of the Holy Spirit.

### What is the deposit of faith?
The deposit of faith is the source of faith that we draw from in order to pass on God's Revelation. The deposit of faith is the unity of Sacred Scripture and Sacred Tradition handed on by the Church from the time of the Apostles.

### What is the Magisterium?
The Magisterium is the teaching authority of the Church. Guided by the Holy Spirit, the Church has the responsibility to authentically and accurately interpret the Word of God, both in Sacred Scripture and in Sacred Tradition. She does this to assure that her understanding of Revelation is faithful to the teaching of the Apostles.

### What is a dogma of faith?
A dogma of faith is a truth taught by the Church as revealed by God and to which we are called to give our assent of mind and heart in faith.

## SACRED SCRIPTURE

### What is Sacred Scripture?
The words *sacred scripture* come from two Latin words meaning "holy writings." Sacred Scripture is the collection of all the writings God has inspired authors to write in his name.

### What is the Bible?
The word *bible* comes from a Greek word meaning "book." The Bible is the collection of the forty-six books of the Old Testament and the twenty-seven books of the New Testament named by the Church as all the writings God has inspired human authors to write in his name.

### What is the canon of Scripture?
The word *canon* comes from a Greek word meaning "measuring rod," or standard by which something is judged. The canon of Scripture is the list of books that the Church has identified and teaches to be the inspired Word of God.

### What is biblical inspiration?
Biblical inspiration is a term that describes the Holy Spirit guiding the human authors of Sacred Scripture so that they faithfully and accurately communicate the Word of God.

### What is the Old Testament?
The Old Testament is the first main part of the Bible. It is the forty-six books inspired by the Holy Spirit, written before the birth of Jesus and centered on the Covenant between God and his people, Israel, and the promise of the Messiah or Savior. The Old Testament is divided into the Torah/Pentateuch, historical books, wisdom literature, and writings of the prophets.

### What is the Torah?
The Torah is the Law of God that was revealed to Moses. The written Torah is found in the first five books of the Old Testament, which are called the "Torah" or the "Pentateuch."

## What is the Pentateuch?

The word *pentateuch* means "five containers." The Pentateuch is the first five books of the Old Testament, namely Genesis, Exodus, Leviticus, Numbers, and Deuteronomy.

## What is the Covenant?

The Covenant is the solemn agreement of fidelity that God and his people freely entered into. It was renewed and fulfilled in Jesus Christ, the new and everlasting Covenant.

## What are the historical books of the Old Testament?

The historical books tell about the fidelity and infidelity of God's people to the Covenant and about the consequences of those choices.

## What are the Wisdom writings of the Old Testament?

The Wisdom writings are the seven books of the Old Testament that contain inspired practical advice and common-sense guidelines for living the Covenant and the Law of God. They are the Book of Job, Book of Psalms, Book of Ecclesiastes, Book of Wisdom, Book of Proverbs, Book of Sirach (Ecclesiasticus), and Song of Songs.

## What are the writings of the prophets in the Old Testament?

The word *prophet* comes from a Greek word meaning "those who speak before others." The biblical prophets were those people God had chosen to speak in his name. The writings of the prophets are the eighteen books of the Old Testament that contain the message of the prophets to God's people. They remind God's people of his unending fidelity to them and of their responsibility to be faithful to the Covenant.

## What is the New Testament?

The New Testament is the second main part of the Bible. It is the twenty-seven books inspired by the Holy Spirit and written in apostolic times that center on Jesus Christ and his saving work among us. The main parts are the four Gospels, the Acts of the Apostles, the twenty-one letters, and the Book of Revelation.

## What are the Gospels?

The word *gospel* comes from a Greek word meaning "good news." The Gospel is the Good News of God's loving plan of Salvation, revealed in the Passion, Death, Resurrection, and Ascension of Jesus Christ. The Gospels are the four written accounts of Matthew, Mark, Luke, and John. The four Gospels occupy a central place in Sacred Scripture because Jesus Christ is their center.

## What is an epistle?

The word *epistle* comes from a Greek word meaning "message or letter." An epistle is a formal type of letter. Some of the letters in the New Testament are epistles.

## What are the Pauline Epistles and letters?

The Pauline Epistles and letters are the fourteen letters in the New Testament traditionally attributed to Saint Paul the Apostle.

## What are the Catholic Letters?

The Catholic Letters are the seven New Testament letters that bear the names of the Apostles John, Peter, Jude, and James, and which were written to the universal Church rather than to a particular Church community.

# THE HOLY TRINITY

## Who is the Mystery of the Holy Trinity?

The Holy Trinity is the mystery of One God in Three Divine Persons—God the Father, God the Son, God the Holy Spirit. It is the central mystery of the Christian faith.

## Who is God the Father?

God the Father is the First Person of the Holy Trinity.

## Who is God the Son?

God the Son is Jesus Christ, the Second Person of the Holy Trinity. He is the Only Begotten Son of the Father who took on flesh and became one of us without giving up his divinity.

## Who is God the Holy Spirit?

God the Holy Spirit is the Third Person of the Holy Trinity, who proceeds from the Father and Son. He is the Advocate, or Paraclete, sent to us by the Father in the name of his Son, Jesus.

## What are the divine missions, or the works of God?

The entire work of God is common to all Three Divine Persons of the Trinity. The work of creation is the work of the Trinity, though attributed to the Father. Likewise, the work of Salvation is attributed to the Son and the work of sanctification is attributed to the Holy Spirit.

# DIVINE WORK OF CREATION

## What is the divine work of creation?

Creation is the work of God bringing into existence everything and everyone, seen and unseen, out of love and without any help.

## Who are angels?

Angels are spiritual creatures who do not have bodies as humans do. Angels give glory to God without ceasing and sometimes serve God by bringing his message to people.

### Who is the human person?

The human person is uniquely created in the image and likeness of God. Human dignity is fulfilled in the vocation to a life of happiness with God.

### What is the soul?

The soul is the spiritual part of a person. It is immortal; it never dies. The soul is the innermost being, that which bears the imprint of the image of God.

### What is the intellect?

The intellect is an essential power of the soul. It is the power to know God, yourself, and others; it is the power to understand the order of things established by God.

### What is free will?

Free will is an essential quality of the soul. It is the God-given ability and power to recognize him as part of our lives and to choose to center our lives around him as well as to choose between good and evil. By free will, the human person is capable of directing oneself toward the truth, beauty and good, namely, life in communion with God.

### What is Original Sin?

Original Sin is the sin of Adam and Eve by which they choose evil over obedience to God. By doing so, they lost the state of original holiness for themselves and for all their descendants. As a result of Original Sin, death, sin, and suffering entered into the world.

## JESUS CHRIST, THE INCARNATE SON OF GOD

### What is the Annunciation?

The Annunciation is the announcement by the angel Gabriel to Mary that God chose her to be the mother of Jesus, the Son of God, by the power of the Holy Spirit.

### What is the Incarnation?

The word *incarnation* comes from a Latin word meaning "take on flesh." The term *Incarnation* is the event in which the Son of God, the Second Person of the Holy Trinity, truly became human while remaining truly God. Jesus Christ is true God and true man.

### What does it mean that Jesus is Lord?

The word *lord* means "master, ruler, a person of authority" and is used in the Old Testament to name God. The designation, or title, "Jesus, the Lord" expresses that Jesus is truly God.

### What is the Paschal Mystery?

The Paschal Mystery is the saving events of the Passion, Death, Resurrection, and glorious Ascension of Jesus Christ; the passing over of Jesus from death into a new and glorious life; the name we give to God's plan of Salvation in Jesus Christ.

### What is Salvation?

The word *salvation* comes from a Latin word meaning "to save." Salvation is the saving, or deliverance, of humanity from the power of sin and death through Jesus Christ. All Salvation comes from Christ through the Church.

### What is the Resurrection?

The Resurrection is the historical event of Jesus being raised from the dead to a new glorified life after his death on the cross and burial in the tomb.

### What is the Ascension?

The Ascension is the return of the Risen Christ in glory to his Father, to the world of the divine.

### What is the Second Coming of Christ?

The Second Coming of Christ is the return of Christ in glory at the end of time to judge the living and the dead; the fulfillment of God's plan in Christ.

### What does it mean that Jesus is the Messiah?

The word *messiah* is a Hebrew term meaning "anointed one." Jesus Christ is the Anointed One, the Messiah, who God promised to send to save people. Jesus is the Savior of the world.

## MYSTERY OF THE CHURCH

### What is the Church?

The word *church* means "convocation," those called together. The Church is the sacrament of Salvation—the sign and instrument of our reconciliation and communion with God the Holy Trinity and with one another. The Church is the Body of Christ, the people God the Father has called together in Jesus Christ through the power of the Holy Spirit.

### What is the central work of the Church?

The central work of the Church is to proclaim the Gospel of Jesus Christ and to invite all people to come to know and believe in him and to live in communion with him. We call this work of the Church "evangelization," a word that comes from a Greek word that means "to tell good news."

### What is the Body of Christ?

The Body of Christ is an image for the Church used by Saint Paul the Apostle that teaches that all the members of the Church are one in Christ, who is the Head of the Church, and that all members have a unique and vital work in the Church.

### Who are the People of God?

The People of God are those the Father has chosen and gathered in Christ, the Incarnate Son of God, the Church. All people are invited to belong to the People of God and to live as one family of God.

## What is the Temple of the Holy Spirit?

The Temple of the Holy Spirit is a New Testament image used to describe the indwelling of the Holy Spirit in the Church and within the hearts of the faithful.

## What is the Communion of Saints?

The Communion of Saints is the communion of holy things and holy people that make up the Church. It is the communion, or unity, of all the faithful, those living on Earth, those being purified after death, and those enjoying life everlasting and eternal happiness with God, the angels, Mary and all the Saints.

## What are the Marks of the Church?

The Marks of the Church are the four attributes and essential characteristics of the Church and her mission, namely, one, holy, catholic, and apostolic.

## Who are the Apostles?

The word *apostle* comes from a Greek word meaning "to send away." The Apostles were those twelve men chosen and sent by Jesus to preach the Gospel and to make disciples of all people.

## Who are the "Twelve"?

The "Twelve" is the term that identifies the Apostles chosen by Jesus before his Death and Resurrection. "The names of the twelve apostles are these: first, Simon called Peter, and his brother Andrew; James, the son of Zebedee, and his brother John; Philip and Bartholomew, Thomas and Matthew the tax collector; James the son of Alphaeus, and Thaddaeus; Simon the Cananean, and Judas Iscariot who betrayed him" (Matthew 10:2–4). The Apostle Matthias was chosen after Jesus' Ascension.

## What is Pentecost?

Pentecost is the coming of the Holy Spirit upon the Church as promised by Jesus; it marks the beginning of the work of the Church.

## Who are the ordained ministers of the Church?

The ordained ministers of the Church are those baptized men who are consecrated in the Sacrament of Holy Orders to serve the whole Church. Bishops, priests, and deacons are the ordained ministers of the Church and make up the clergy.

## How do the pope and other bishops guide the Church in her work?

Christ, the Head of the Church, governs the Church through the Pope and the college of bishops in communion with him. The Pope is the bishop of Rome and the successor of Saint Peter the Apostle. The Pope, the Vicar of Christ, is the visible foundation of the unity of the whole Church. The other bishops are the successors of the other Apostles and are the visible foundation of their own particular Churches. The Holy Spirit guides the Pope and the college of bishops working together with the Pope, to teach the faith and moral doctrine without error. This grace of the Holy Spirit is called *infallibility*.

## What is the consecrated life?

The consecrated life is a state of life for those baptized who promise or vow to live the Gospel by means of professing the evangelical counsels of poverty, chastity, and obedience, in a way of life approved by the Church. The consecrated life is also known as the "religious life."

## Who are the laity?

The laity (or laypeople) are all the baptized who have not received the Sacrament of Holy Orders nor have promised or vowed to live the consecrated life. They are called to be witnesses to Christ at the very heart of the human community.

# THE BLESSED VIRGIN MARY

## What is Mary's role in God's loving plan for humanity?

Mary has a unique role in God's plan of Salvation for humanity. For this reason she is full of grace from the first moment of her conception, or existence. God chose Mary to be the mother of the Incarnate Son of God, Jesus Christ, who is truly God and truly man. Mary is the Mother of God, the Mother of Christ, and the Mother of the Church. She is the greatest Saint of the Church.

## What is the Immaculate Conception?

The Immaculate Conception is the unique grace given to Mary that totally preserved her from the stain of all sin from the very first moment of her existence, or conception, in her mother's womb and throughout her life.

## What is the perpetual virginity of Mary?

The *perpetual virginity of Mary* is a term that describes the fact that Mary remained always a virgin. She was virgin before the conception of Jesus, during his birth, and remained a virgin after the birth of Jesus her whole life.

## What is the Assumption of Mary?

At the end of her life on Earth, the Blessed Virgin Mary was taken body and soul into Heaven, where she shares in the glory of her Son's Resurrection. Mary, the Mother of the Church, hears our prayers and intercedes for us with her Son. She is an image of the heavenly glory in which we all hope to share when Christ, her Son, comes again in glory.

# LIFE EVERLASTING

## What is eternal life?

Eternal life is life after death. At death the soul is separated from the body. In the Apostles' Creed we profess faith in "the life everlasting." In the Nicene Creed we profess faith in "the life of the world to come."

## What is the particular judgment?
The particular judgment is the assignment given to our souls at the moment of our death to our final destiny based on what we have done in our lives.

## What is the Last Judgment?
The Last Judgment is the judgment at which every human being will appear in their own bodies and give an account of their deeds. At the Last Judgment, Christ will show his identity with the least of his brothers and sisters.

## What is the beatific vision?
The beatific vision is seeing God "face-to-face" in heavenly glory.

## What is Heaven?
Heaven is eternal life and communion with the Holy Trinity. It is the supreme state of happiness—living with God forever for which he created us.

## What is the Kingdom of God?
The Kingdom of God, or Kingdom of Heaven, is the image used by Jesus to describe all people and creation living in communion with God. The Kingdom of God will be fully realized when Christ comes again in glory at the end of time.

## What is Purgatory?
Purgatory is the opportunity after death to purify and strengthen our love for God before we enter Heaven.

## What is hell?
Hell is the immediate and everlasting separation from God.

# LITURGY AND WORSHIP

## What is worship?
Worship is the adoration and honor given to God. The Church worships God publicly in the celebration of the liturgy. The liturgy is the Church's worship of God. It is the work of the whole Church. In the liturgy the mystery of Salvation in Christ is made present by the power of the Holy Spirit.

## What is the liturgical year?
The liturgical year is the cycle of seasons and great feasts that make up the Church's year of worship. The main seasons and times of the Church year are Advent, Christmas, Lent, Easter Triduum, Easter, and Ordinary Time.

# THE SACRAMENTS

## What are the Sacraments?
The Sacraments are seven signs of God's love and the main liturgical actions of the Church through which the faithful are made sharers in the Paschal Mystery of Christ. They are effective signs of grace, instituted by Christ and entrusted to the Church, by which divine life is shared with us.

## What are the Sacraments of Christian Initiation?
The Sacraments of Christian Initiation are Baptism, Confirmation, and the Eucharist. These three Sacraments are the foundation of every Christian life. "Baptism is the beginning of new life in Christ; Confirmation is its strengthening; the Eucharist nourishes the faithful for their transformation into Christ."

## What is the Sacrament of Baptism?
Through Baptism we are reborn into new life in Christ. We are joined to Jesus Christ, become members of the Church, and are reborn as God's children. We receive the gift of the Holy Spirit; and Original Sin and our personal sins are forgiven. Baptism marks us indelibly and forever as belonging to Christ. Because of this, Baptism can be received only once.

## What is the Sacrament of Confirmation?
Confirmation strengthens the graces of Baptism and celebrates the special gift of the Holy Spirit. Confirmation also imprints a spiritual or indelible character on the soul and can be received only once.

## What is the Sacrament of the Eucharist?
The Eucharist is the source and summit of the Christian life. In the Eucharist the faithful join with Christ to give thanksgiving, honor, and glory to the Father through the power of the Holy Spirit. Through the power of the Holy Spirit and the words of the priest, the bread and wine become the Body and Blood of Christ.

## What is the obligation of the faithful to participate in the Eucharist?
The faithful have the obligation to participate in the Eucharist on Sundays and holy days of obligation. Sunday is the Lord's Day. Sunday, the day of the Lord's Resurrection, is "the foundation and kernel of the whole liturgical year." Regular participation in the Eucharist and receiving Holy Communion is vital to the Christian life. In the Eucharist we receive the Body and Blood of Christ.

## What is the Blessed Sacrament?
The Blessed Sacrament is another name for the Eucharist. The term is often used to identify the Eucharist reserved in the tabernacle.

## What is the Mass?

The Mass is the main celebration of the Church at which we gather to listen to the Word of God (Liturgy of the Word) and through which we are made sharers in the saving Death and Resurrection of Christ and give praise and glory to the Father (Liturgy of the Eucharist).

## What are the Sacraments of Healing?

Penance and Reconciliation and Anointing of the Sick are the two Sacraments of Healing. Through the power of the Holy Spirit, Christ's work of Salvation and healing of the members of the Church is continued.

## What is the Sacrament of Penance and Reconciliation?

The Sacrament of Penance and Reconciliation is one of the two Sacraments of Healing through which we receive God's forgiveness for the sins we have committed after Baptism.

## What is confession?

Confession is the telling of sins to a priest in the Sacrament of Penance and Reconciliation. This act of the penitent is an essential element of the Sacrament. Confession is also another name for the Sacrament of Penance and Reconciliation.

## What is the seal of confession?

The seal of confession is the obligation of the priest to never reveal to anyone what a penitent has confessed to him.

## What is contrition?

Contrition is sorrow for sins that includes the desire and commitment to make reparation for the harm caused by one's sin and the purpose of amendment not to sin again. Contrition is an essential element of the Sacrament of Penance and Reconciliation.

## What is a penance?

A penance is a prayer or act of kindness that shows we are truly sorry for our sins and that helps us repair the damage caused by our sin. Accepting and doing our penance is an essential part of the Sacrament of Penance and Reconciliation.

## What is absolution?

Absolution is the forgiveness of sins by God through the ministry of the priest.

## What is the Sacrament of Anointing of the Sick?

The Sacrament of Anointing of the Sick is one of the two Sacraments of Healing. The grace of this Sacrament strengthens our faith and trust in God when we are seriously ill, weakened by old age, or dying. The faithful may receive this Sacrament each time they are seriously ill or when an illness gets worse.

## What is Viaticum?

Viaticum is the Eucharist, or Holy Communion, received as food and strength for a dying person's journey from life on Earth through death to eternal life.

## What are the Sacraments at the Service of Communion?

Holy Orders and Matrimony are the two Sacraments at the Service of Communion. These Sacraments bestow a particular work, or mission, on certain members of the Church to serve in building up the People of God.

## What is the Sacrament of Holy Orders?

The Sacrament of Holy Orders is one of the two Sacraments at the Service of Communion. It is the Sacrament in which baptized men are consecrated as bishops, priests, or deacons to serve the whole Church in the name and person of Christ.

## Who is a bishop?

A bishop is a priest who receives the fullness of the Sacrament of Holy Orders. He is a successor of the Apostles and shepherds a particular Church entrusted to him by means of teaching, leading divine worship, and governing the Church as Jesus did.

## Who is a priest?

A priest is a baptized man who has received the Sacrament of Holy Orders. Priests are coworkers with their bishops, who have the ministry of authentically teaching the faith, celebrating divine worship, above all the Eucharist, and guiding their churches as true pastors.

## Who is a deacon?

A deacon is ordained to assist bishops and priests. He is not ordained to the priesthood but to a ministry of service to the Church.

## What is the Sacrament of Matrimony?

The Sacrament of Matrimony is one of the two Sacraments at the Service of Communion. In the Sacrament of Matrimony a baptized man and a baptized woman dedicate their lives to the Church and to one another in a lifelong bond of faithful life-giving love. In this Sacrament they receive the grace to be a living sign of Christ's love for the Church.

## What are the sacramentals of the Church?

Sacramentals are sacred signs instituted by the Church. They include blessings, prayers, and certain objects that prepare us to participate in the Sacraments and make us aware of and help us respond to God's loving presence in our lives.

## THE MORAL LIFE

### Why was the human person created?

The human person was created to give honor and glory to God and to live a life of beatitude with God here on Earth and forever in Heaven.

### What is the Christian moral life?

The baptized have new life in Christ in the Holy Spirit. They respond to the "desire for happiness that God has placed in every human heart by cooperating with the grace of the Holy Spirit and living the Gospel. The moral life is a spiritual worship that finds its nourishment in the liturgy and celebration of the Sacraments."

### What is the way to happiness revealed by Jesus Christ?

Jesus taught that the Great Commandment of loving God above all else and our neighbor as ourselves is the path to happiness. It is the summary and heart of the Commandments and all of God's Law.

### What are the Ten Commandments?

The Ten Commandments are the laws of the Covenant that God revealed to Moses and the Israelites on Mount Sinai. The Ten Commandments are also known as the Decalogue, or "Ten Words." They are the "privileged expression of the natural law," which is written on the hearts of all people.

### What are the Beatitudes?

The Beatitudes are the teachings of Jesus that summarize the path to true happiness, the Kingdom of God, which is living in communion and friendship with God, and with Mary and all the Saints. The Beatitudes guide us in living as disciples of Christ by keeping our life focused and centered on God.

### What is the New Commandment?

The New Commandment is the Commandment of love that Jesus gave his disciples. Jesus said, "I give you a new commandment: love one another. As I have loved you, so you also should love one another" (John 13:34).

### What are the Works of Mercy?

The word *mercy* comes from a Hebrew word pointing to God's unconditional love and kindness at work in the world. Human works of mercy are acts of loving kindness by which we reach out to people in their corporal and spiritual needs.

### What are the precepts of the Church?

Precepts of the Church are specific responsibilities that concern the moral Christian life united with the liturgy and nourished by it.

## HOLINESS OF LIFE

### What is holiness?

Holiness is the state of living in communion with God. It designates both the presence of God, the Holy One, with us and our faithfulness to him. It is the characteristic of a person who is in right relationship with God, with people, and with creation.

### What is grace?

Grace is the gift of God sharing his life and love with us. Categories of grace are sanctifying grace, actual grace, charisms, and sacramental graces.

### What is sanctifying grace?

The word *sanctifying* comes from a Latin word meaning "to make holy." Sanctifying grace is a gratuitous gift of God, given by the Holy Spirit, as a remedy for sin and the source of holiness.

### What is actual grace?

Actual graces are the God-given divine helps empowering us to live as his adopted daughters and sons.

### What are charisms?

Charisms are gifts or graces freely given to individual Christians by the Holy Spirit for the benefit of building up the Church.

### What are sacramental graces?

Sacramental graces are the graces of each of the Sacraments that help us live out our Christian vocation.

### What are the Gifts of the Holy Spirit?

The seven Gifts of the Holy Spirit are graces that strengthen us to live our Baptism, our new life in Christ. They are wisdom, understanding, right judgment (or counsel), courage (or fortitude), knowledge, reverence (or piety), wonder and awe (or fear of the Lord).

### What are the Fruits of the Holy Spirit?

The twelve Fruits of the Holy Spirit are visible signs and effects of the Holy Spirit at work in our life. They are charity (love), joy, peace, patience, kindness, goodness, generosity, gentleness, faithfulness, modesty, self-control, and chastity.

## THE VIRTUES

### What are virtues?

The virtues are spiritual powers or habits or behaviors that help us do what is good. The Catholic Church speaks of Theological Virtues, Moral Virtues, and Cardinal Virtues.

## What are the Theological Virtues?

The Theological Virtues are the three virtues of faith, hope, and charity (love). These virtues are "gifts from God infused into the souls of the faithful to make them capable of acting as his children and of attaining eternal life" (CCC 1813).

## What are the Moral Virtues?

The Moral Virtues are "firm attitudes, stable dispositions, habitual perfections of intellect and will that govern our actions, order our passions, and guide our conduct according to reason and faith. They make possible ease, self-mastery, and joy in leading a morally good life" (CCC 1804).

## What are the Cardinal Virtues?

The Cardinal Virtues are the four Moral Virtues of prudence, justice, fortitude, and temperance. They are called the Cardinal Virtues because all of the Moral Virtues are related to and grouped around them.

## What is conscience?

The word *conscience* comes from a Latin word meaning "to be conscious of guilt." Conscience is that part of every human person that helps us judge whether a moral act is in accordance or not in accordance with God's Law; our conscience moves us to do good and avoid evil.

# MORAL EVIL AND SIN

## What is moral evil?

Moral evil is the harm we willingly inflict on one another and on God's good creation.

## What is temptation?

Temptation is everything, either within us or outside us, that tries to move us from doing something good that we know we can and should do and to do or say something we know is contrary to the will of God. Temptation is whatever tries to move us away from living a holy life.

## What is sin?

Sin is freely and knowingly doing or saying that which is against the will of God and the Law of God. Sin sets itself against God's love and turns our hearts away from his love. The Church speaks of mortal sin, venial sin, and Capital Sins.

## What is mortal sin?

A mortal sin is a serious, deliberate failure in our love and respect for God, our neighbor, creation, and ourselves. It is knowingly and willingly choosing to do something that is gravely contrary to the Law of God. The effect of mortal sin is the loss of sanctifying grace and, if unrepented, mortal sin brings eternal death.

## What are venial sins?

Venial sins are sins that are less serious than a mortal sin. They weaken our love for God and for one another and diminish our holiness.

## What are Capital Sins?

Capital sins are sins that are at the root of other sins. The seven Capital Sins are false pride, avarice, envy, anger, gluttony, lust, and sloth.

# CHRISTIAN PRAYER

## What is prayer?

Prayer is conversation with God. It is talking and listening to him, raising our minds and hearts to God the Father, Son, and Holy Spirit.

## What is the prayer of all Christians?

The Lord's Prayer, or Our Father, is the prayer of all Christians. It is the prayer Jesus taught his disciples and gave to the Church. The Lord's Prayer is "a summary of the whole Gospel." Praying the Lord's Prayer "brings us into communion with the Father and his Son, Jesus Christ" and develops "in us the will to become like [Jesus] and to place our trust in the Father as he did" (CCC 2763).

## What are the traditional expressions of prayer?

The traditional expressions of prayer are vocal prayer, the prayer of meditation, and the prayer of contemplation.

## What is vocal prayer?

Vocal prayer is spoken prayer; prayer using words said aloud.

## What is the prayer of meditation?

Meditation is a form of prayer in which we use our minds, hearts, imaginations, emotions, and desires to understand and follow what the Lord is asking us to do.

## What is the prayer of contemplation?

Contemplation is a form of prayer that is simply being with God.

## What are the traditional forms of prayer?

The traditional forms of prayer are the prayers of adoration and blessing, the prayer of thanksgiving, the prayer of praise, the prayer of petition, and the prayer of intercession.

## What are devotions?

Devotions are part of the prayer life of the Church and of the baptized. They are acts of communal or individual prayer that surround and arise out of the celebration of the liturgy.

# BOOKS of the BIBLE

## The Old Testament

### Law (Torah) or Pentateuch

| | |
|---|---|
| Genesis | (Gn) |
| Exodus | (Ex) |
| Leviticus | (Lv) |
| Numbers | (Nm) |
| Deuteronomy | (Dt) |

### Historical Books

| | |
|---|---|
| Joshua | (Jos) |
| Judges | (Jgs) |
| Ruth | (Ru) |
| First Book of Samuel | (1 Sm) |
| Second Book of Samuel | (2 Sm) |
| First Book of Kings | (1 Kgs) |
| Second Book of Kings | (2 Kgs) |
| First Book of Chronicles | (1 Chr) |
| Second Book of Chronicles | (2 Chr) |
| Ezra | (Ezr) |
| Nehemiah | (Neh) |
| Tobit | (Tb) |
| Judith | (Jdt) |
| Esther | (Est) |
| First Book of Maccabees | (1 Mc) |
| Second Book of Maccabees | (2 Mc) |

### Poetry and Wisdom Books

| | |
|---|---|
| Job | (Jb) |
| Psalms | (Ps) |
| Proverbs | (Prv) |
| Ecclesiastes | (Eccl) |
| Song of Songs | (Sg) |
| Wisdom | (Wis) |
| Sirach/Ecclesiasticus | (Sir) |

### Prophets

| | |
|---|---|
| Isaiah | (Is) |
| Jeremiah | (Jer) |
| Lamentations | (Lam) |
| Baruch | (Bar) |
| Ezekiel | (Ez) |
| Daniel | (Dn) |
| Hosea | (Hos) |
| Joel | (Jl) |
| Amos | (Am) |
| Obadiah | (Ob) |
| Jonah | (Jon) |
| Micah | (Mi) |
| Nahum | (Na) |
| Habakkuk | (Hb) |
| Zephaniah | (Zep) |
| Haggai | (Hg) |
| Zechariah | (Zec) |
| Malachi | (Mal) |

## The New Testament

### The Gospels

| | |
|---|---|
| Matthew | (Mt) |
| Mark | (Mk) |
| Luke | (Lk) |
| John | (Jn) |

### Early Church

| | |
|---|---|
| Acts of the Apostles | (Acts) |

### Letters of Paul and Other Letters

| | |
|---|---|
| Romans | (Rom) |
| First Letter to the Corinthians | (1 Cor) |
| Second Letter to the Corinthians | (2 Cor) |
| Galatians | (Gal) |
| Ephesians | (Eph) |
| Philippians | (Phil) |
| Colossians | (Col) |
| First Letter to the Thessalonians | (1 Thes) |
| Second Letter to the Thessalonians | (2 Thes) |
| First Letter to Timothy | (1 Tm) |
| Second Letter to Timothy | (2 Tm) |
| Titus | (Ti) |
| Philemon | (Phlm) |
| Hebrews | (Heb) |
| James | (Jas) |
| First Letter of Peter | (1 Pt) |
| Second Letter of Peter | (2 Pt) |
| First Letter of John | (1 Jn) |
| Second Letter of John | (2 Jn) |
| Third Letter of John | (3 Jn) |
| Jude | (Jude) |

### Revelation

| | |
|---|---|
| Revelation | (Rv) |

# GLOSSARY

## A — B

**abortion** *page 114*

Direct abortion is the intentional killing of a child conceived but not yet born; that is, an unborn human person who is still living in the mother's womb.

**actual grace** *page 27*

This type of grace is the divine help empowering us to live as God's adopted daughters and sons.

**adultery** *page 125*

The voluntary act of a married person engaging in sexual intercourse with someone other than his or her spouse is adultery. This act violates the dignity of marriage.

**blasphemy** *page 103*

The act of claiming to be God, having divine attributes, or showing contempt for God is blasphemy.

## C — D

**Cardinal Virtues** *page 60*

These good habits are those on which all good human acts hinge upon. They are prudence, justice, fortitude, and temperance.

**catholic** *page 14*

The word catholic means "universal." This is one of the four essential charactertics or Marks of the Church.

**chastity** *page 124*

The appropriate and successful integration of the gift of sexuality within the whole person in accord with his or her vocational state of life. Chastity is one of the twelve Fruits of the Holy Spirit.

**common good** *page 62*

This principle of Catholic Social Teaching is the ultimate good each and every member of society has been created to achieve. The common good is when every person within a given group has their needs taken care of and their rights protected.

**conscience** *page 52*

God has given each of us a gift to help us judge right from wrong. This gift is called the conscience.

**covet** *page 138*

To want or desire what belongs to another is to covet. This might include wrongfully desiring another's possessions, abilities, talents, friends, achievements, etc.

**dignity** *page 38*

God created every human person in his image and likeness. Because of this, each of us has an inherent quality of worthiness called dignity.

**discipleship** *page 36*

A disciple is one who learns from and follows a teacher. Christian discipleship is learning and following Jesus Christ, our teacher. As his disciples, we place total and unconditional trust in God the Father as Christ did.

## E — F — G — H

**ecumenical council** *page 88*

This universal gathering of the bishops is called by the Pope or approved by him in the exercise of their collegial authority to shepherd the Church.

**envy** *page 138*

This is the state of feeling angry or saddened that other people have something you do not have. Envy is one of the seven Captial Sins.

**euthanasia** *page 115*

The direct killing of a person who is suffering from a long-term or even terminal illness is euthanasia.

**evangelization** *page 12*

The announcement or proclamation of the Gospel by words and deeds. This main work of the Church teaches as Jesus taught and fulfills his command to make disciples of all nations.

**free will** *page 25*

The ability and power given to us by God to choose between good and evil is free will. God created us to use our free will to recognize him as part of our lives and to choose to center our lives around him.

**generosity** *page 140*

The capacity, quality, or activity of giving or sharing of oneself or what one has abundantly, beyond one's basic needs is generosity.

**grace** *page 72*

The gift of God sharing his life with us is called grace.

**hedonism** *page 124*

A way of thinking and living that places the pursuit of pleasure as the top priority is called hedonism.

**holiness** *page 25*

Holiness refers to God's presence with us and our faithfulness to him. In living one's life in Christ, a holy person is in right relationship with God.

## I — J — K — L

**idols** *page 102*

Anything that takes the place of God in our lives are false gods or idols.

**integrity** *page 136*

Being true to the person God created one to be, seeking only what is true, beautiful, and good about God, oneself, others, and the world is having integrity.

**intellect** *page 25*

God created us with this power to know him, others, and ourselves. The intellect enables us to reflect on how God is part of our lives.

**justification** *page 75*

This gift of new life in Christ places us in right relationship with God. We receive this through sanctifying grace at Baptism.

**Kingdom of God** *page 36*

This is the biblical image for eternal life with God. God's Kingdom describes the eternal communion between God and all of creation, and will be complete at the end of time when Christ comes again in glory.

**laity** *page 89*

Those baptized members of the Church who have not received Ordination nor promised to live the consecrated life are part of the laity of the Church, or laypeople.

**lying** *page 136*

The act of intentionally deceiving another person by deliberately saying what is false or withholding the truth from someone who has the right to know that truth is lying.

## M — N — O — P

**merit** *page 76*

To be worthy of or deserve is to merit.

**missionaries** *page 10*

A missionary is a Christian who travels to places around the world to live and preach the Gospel.

**morality** *page 48*

This term describes the means of understanding whether our intentional actions are good or evil.

**natural law** *page 50*

The sense of knowing good and evil by use of human reason is called the natural law. This is the universal foundation of moral life for each person.

**obedience** *page 112*

The act of respectful listening and trusting response to a person of authority is obedience. When we are asked to do something that is in accordance with God's Law or a just civil law, we have the obligation to obey that law.

**perjury** *page 103*

The act of intentionally breaking an oath or promise by speaking falsely or by omitting the truth is perjury.

**reverence** *page 103*

The attitude of awe, profound respect, and love for someone or for God is reverence. Reverence for God is related to piety, one of the seven Gifts of the Holy Spirit.

**sanctification** *page 75*

This work of the Holy Spirit makes us holy. Sanctification unites us by faith to the Paschal Mystery. We become sharers of God's life through the work of the Holy Spirit.

**sanctifying grace** *page 24*

This type of grace is the gift of God's life and love with us, making us holy. This grace enable us to live in communion with the Holy Trinity.

**sin** *page 49*

This is the act of freely and knowingly doing or saying what we know is against God's Law. Sin sets us against God's love and turns our hearts away from him.

**solidarity** *page 90*

This principle of Catholic Social Teaching is the unification of all members of society, or of people in a particular group.

**soul** *page 24*

The soul is the spiritual part of who we are that is immortal; our innermost being, which bears the imprint of the image of God.

**stewardship** *page 126*

The actions of responsibly caring for what God has given to us is called stewardship. When we care for gift of creation, we are acting as responsible stewards.

**temptation** *page 152*

Anything that tries to move us to do or say something we know is wrong or from doing something good we know we can or ought to do is a temptation. Tempations keep us from living holy lives.

**Theological Virtues** *page 60*

These good habits are strengths given to us by God to help us attain holiness. They are faith, hope, and charity.

# INDEX

# CREDITS

**Cover Illustration: Gerad Taylor**

**Photography Credits**
**Frontmatter:** Page 3, (tr) © Bill Wittman; (bl) © Fuse/Getty Images; 4, © Cultura Creative/Alamy; 5, (tr) © Stargazer/Shutterstock; (c) © Bill Wittman; (bl) © Kablonk/SuperStock; 6, © Wojciech Wojcik/Alamy.
**Chapter 1:** Page 9, © Robert Harding Picture Library Ltd/Alamy; 10, © Borderlands/Alamy; 11, (tr) © Thomas Kokta/Getty Images; (cr) © Maryknoll Sisters Photo Library; 13, © Look and Learn/The Bridgeman Art Library; 14, (t) © Bill Wittman; (bl) © Peter Barritt/Alamy; 15, (cr) © Andre Nantel/Shutterstock; (b) © Moment/Getty Images; 16, © Friedrich Stark/Alamy; 17, (bkgd) © Ocean/Corbis; (b) © David Grossman/Getty Images; 18, (bkgd) © Philippe Lissac/Godong/Corbis; (inset) © Ray Laskowitz/Getty Images; 20, (bkgd) © Bill Wittman.
**Chapter 2:** Page 21, (bkgd) © Digital Vision/Getty Images; 22, (inset) © Bernard Weil/Toronto Star/ZUMAPRESS/Newscom; (bkgd) © AL.COM/Landov; 23, © Bernard Weil/Toronto St/ZUMA Press/Newscom; 24, © INSADCO Photography/Alamy; 25, (tl) © Rafael Ben-Ari/Alamy; (cr) © Design Pics Inc./Alamy; 26, (bl) © AP Photo/Archdiocese of Detroit; (bc) © Zvonimir Atletic /shutterstock; 27, (tr) © Keith Dannemiller/Alamy; 28, (tl) © Jim West/Alamy; 29, (bkgd) © Tim Pannell/Corbis; (br) © Thinkstock/Getty Images; 30, (bkgd) © B Christopher/Alamy; 31, (br)© Andy Dean Photography/Alamy; 32, (bkgd) © Svabo/Alamy.
**Chapter 3:** Page 33, © JGI/Jamie Grill/Getty Images; 34, © Karl Grobl/ZUMAPRESS/Newscom; 35, ©Carlos Mora/Alamy; 37, © Flavia Maria PERRONE/Gamma-Rapho via Getty Images; 38, © Art Directors & TRIP/Alamy; 39, (t) © Moment/cultura/Corbis; (cr) © MIXA/Alamy; 40, © TIM GRAHAM/Alamy; 41, (bkgd) © Erik Isakson/Getty Images; (br) © Paul Simcock/Getty Images; 42, (bkgd) © Michael Pole/CORBIS; (cr) © Monalyn Gracia/Corbis; 43, © Seth Wenig/Star Ledger/Corbis; 44, © KidStock/Getty Images.
**Chapter 4:** Page 45, © Galyna Andrushko/Shutterstock; 46, © Alex Bowie/Getty Images; 47, © AP Photo; 48, © Design Pics Inc./Alamy; 49, (t) © Bill Wittman; (cr)©Leila Cutler/Alamy; 50, (tl) ©J.D.S/Shutterstock; (bl) © INSADCO Photography/Alamy; (cl) © Ivy Close Images/Alamy; 51, (cr) © David Grossman/Alamy; (t) © Ingram Publishing/Alamy; 52, © Antonello Nusca/Polaris/Newscom; 53, (br) © Andresr/Shutterstock; (c) © Bill Wittman; 54, © Steve Skjold/Alamy; 55, © Ron Chapple Stock/Alamy; 56, © Bob Daemmrich/Photo Edit.
**Chapter 5:** Page 57, © Fotokostic/Shutterstock; 59, (tl) © Philippe Lissac/GODONG/picture-alliance/Newscom; (cr) © mangostock/Shutterstock; 60, © Krasowit/Shutterstock; 61, (tc) © Lebrecht Music and Arts Photo Library/Alamy; (tl) © ZUMA Press, Inc./Alamy; (tl) © Stan Pritchard/Alamy; (tc) © The Art Gallery Collection/Alamy; (cr) © IS2 from Image Source/Alamy; 62, © Blend Images/Alamy; 63, (cr) © Lisa F. Young/Shutterstock; (t) © CHUCK KENNEDY/KRT/Newscom; 64, © cubrazol/Shutterstock; 65, (br) © Steve Skjold/Alamy; (bkgd) © Jeff Greenberg/Alamy; 66, (bkgd) © Lisa Peardon/Getty Images; (cr) © Michael Novelo/Alamy; 67, © Jim West/Alamy; 68, © Thomas Northcut/Getty Images.
**Chapter 6:** Page 69, © BrankaVV/Shutterstock; 70, (tl) © Bill Wittman; (bkgd) © Bill Wittman; 71, (cr) © David Grossman/Alamy; 72, © The Protected Art Archive/Alamy; 73, (t) © Bill Wittman; (cr) © Bogdan VASILESCU/Shutterstock; 74, © Golden Pixels LLC/Shutterstock; 76, © Fuse/Getty Images; 77, (br) © Jim West/Alamy; (bkgd) © Purestock/Alamy; 78, (tl) © Image Source/Alamy; (bkgd) StockbrokerXtra/Alamy; 79, © Ocean/Corbis; 80, © Elena Itsenko/Shutterstock.
**Chapter 7:** Page 85, © Big Cheese Photo LLC/Alamy; 86, (bkgd) © AP Photo/Luigi Felici; (cl) © Mondadori Collection/UIG Universal Images Group/Newscom; 87, © Universal Images Group/DeAgostini/Alamy; 88, © Bill Wittman; 89, (cr) © Gari Wyn Williams/Alamy; (t) © ZUMA Wire Service/Alamy; 91, (cr) © CPP/Polaris/Newscom; 92, © SUCHETA DAS/Reuters/Corbis; 93, (br) © Bill Wittman; (bkgd) © Bill Wittman; 94, © Rana Faure/Corbis; 95, © Golden Pixels LLC/Alamy; 96, © Bill Wittman.

**Chapter 8:** Page 97, © Fer Gregory/Shutterstock; 98, © Bill Wittman; 99, © JLP/Jose L. Pelaez/Corbis; 101, (cr) © Zvonimir Atletic /Shutterstock; (t) © Bill Wittman; 102, © Blend Images/Alamy; 103, (t) © George Muresan/Shutterstock; (r) © tipograffias/Shutterstock; 104, © Melanie Stetson Freeman/The Christian Science Monitor via Getty Images; 105, (bkgd) © Blend Images/Alamy; 105, (inset) © Africa Studio/Shutterstock; 106, (bkgd) © Anna Omelchenko/Shutterstock; (inset) © Erik Isakson/Blend Images/Corbis; 107, © iStockphoto/Thinkstock; 108, ©Zvonimir Atletic /Shutterstock.
**Chapter 9:** Page 109, © Siri Stafford/Thinkstock; (bkgd) ©LilKar/Shutterstock; 110, (bkgd) ©CLAUDIO PERI/EPA/Newscom; (inset) ©HENNING KAISER/AFP/Getty Images/Newscom; 111, (cr) © CLAUDIO ONORATI/EPA/Newscom; 113, (b) ©Tom Grill/Corbis; (cr) © Bill Stormont/CORBIS; 114, (cl) © iStockphoto/Thinkstock; (bl) © ZUMA Wire Service/Alamy; 115, (t) © Dennis MacDonald/Photo Edit; (br) © Yuri Arcurs/Alamy; 116, © Design Pics Inc./Alamy; 117, (inset) © Image Source/Alamy; (bkgd) Image Source/Alamy; 118, © Kladej/Shutterstock; 119, © Brand X Pictures/Thinkstock; 120, © Olivia Bell Photography/Getty Images.
**Chapter 10:** Page 121, © Drew Myers/Corbis; 122, © Mike P Shepherd/Alamy; 123, © Thinkstock; 124, © Monkey Business Images/Shutterstock; 125, © Purestock/Alamy; 126, © Bill Wittman; 128, © Digital Vision/Thinkstock; 129, (bkgd) © Creatas/Thinkstock; (b) © Jean Valley/Shutterstock; 130, © Photodisc/Thinkstock; 131, © Wave Royalty Free/Design Pics Inc/Alamy; 132, © Jeff Morgan 04/Alamy.
**Chapter 11:** Page 133, © ZUMA Wire Service/Alamy; 134, © SuperStock/Glowimages; 135, (tl) © Art Directors & TRIP/Alamy; (cr) © INTERFOTO/Alamy; 136, © Hola Images/Alamy; 137, © Brand X Pictures/Thinkstock; 139, (cl) © Jenny Acheson/Getty Images; (b) © Kevin Dodge/Corbis; (c) © Jupiterimages/Thinkstock; 140, (t) © Krivosheev Vitaly/Shutterstock; (inset) © iStockphoto/Thinkstock; 141, (inset) © RonTech2000/Getty Images; (bkgd) © Stefano Stefani/Getty Images; 142, (bkgd) © Design Pics Inc./Alamy; (inset) © Tim Pannell/Corbis; 143, © Radius Images/Alamy; 144, © Bill Wittman.
**Chapter 12:** Page 145, © WDG Photo/Shutterstock; 146, © De Agostini Picture Library/The Bridgeman Art Library; 147, (tl) © The Bridgeman Art Library Ltd./Alamy; (cr) akg-images/Gerhard Ruf/Newscom; 149, © Bill Wittman; 150, © NASA, ESA, and the Hubble Heritage; 151, © Bill Wittman; 152, © Odua Images/Shutterstock; 153, © Bill Wittman; 154, © Sean Justice/Corbis; 155, © iStockphoto/Thinkstock; 156, © Sebastien Desarmaux/Corbis.
**Backmatter:** Page 160, © Zvonimir Atletic/Alamy; 161, © Tim Pannell/Corbis; 162, © Look and Learn/The Bridgeman Art Library; 166, © James Shaffer/Photo Edit; 167, © Bill Wittman; 168, © Bill Wittman; 169, © Bill Wittman.

**Illustration Credits**
**Unit 1 Opener:** Page 7, Gerad Taylor
**Chapter 1:** Page 12, Anton Petrov
**Chapter 2:** Page 27, Anton Petrov
**Chapter 3:** Page 36, Gustavo Mazali
**Chapter 5:** Page 58, Anton Petrov
**Chapter 6:** Page 75, Fabio Leone
**Unit 2 Opener:** Page 83, Gerad Taylor
**Chapter 7:** Page 90, Leonardo Meschini
**Chapter 8:** Page 100, Fabio Leone
**Chapter 9:** Page 112, Anton Petrov
**Chapter 10:** Page 126, Fabio Leone
**Chapter 12:** Page 148, Fabio Leone